Natural Stonescapes

The Art and Craft of Stone Placement

Richard L. Dubé, APLD,
and Frederick C. Campbell

STOREY
BOOKS

The mission of Storey Communications is to serve our customers by publishing practical information that encourages personal independence in harmony with the environment.

Edited by Julia Rubel and Nancy Ringer
Cover design by Meredith Maker and Mark Tomasi
Front and back cover photographs © Maggie Oster
Text design by Mark Tomasi
Text production by Mark Tomasi and Jen Rork
Photographs credited on page 167
Line drawings by Rick Daskam
Indexed by Hagerty & Holloway

Storey Books are available for special premium and promotional uses and for customized editions. For further information, please call Storey's Custom Publishing Department at 1-800-793-9396.

Printed in Canada by Transcontinental Printing
10 9 8 7 6 5 4 3 2

Library of Congress Cataloging-in-Publication Data

Dubé, Richard L.
      Natural Stonescapes : the art and craft of stone placement /
Richard L. Dubé and Frederick C. Campbell
          p.   cm.
      Includes index.
      ISBN 1-58017-092-7 (pbk. : alk. paper)
        1. Stone in landscape gardening.   I. Campbell, Frederick C.,
1951– . II. Title.
SB475.5.D83   1999
717—dc21   98-31046
                                        CIP

Dedication

To my wife, for her support, patience, and tolerance: This book should help to answer her standing question, "Don't you have enough pictures of rocks?"

— Richard L. Dubé

To my loving wife, Jane, who endured years of trips, detours, and quick stops to admire stone. Also to my four children, Stephanie, Drew, Chace, and Katrina, who each in their own turn spent Saturday mornings looking at the yards of prospective clients. Lastly to God, who made the stones I admire and whose grace allows me to participate with one of the finest stone designers and friends this man could have.

— Frederick C. Campbell

Contents

Introduction

It would be hard to count the number of times we have seen planting beds or hillsides filled to overflowing with beautiful perennials, ground covers, evergreens, annuals, and bulbs. Unfortunately, ornamentation of the landscape too often seems to be very single-minded. Although they can be strikingly beautiful, in almost every case the plantings could be significantly enhanced by the addition of just one simple item. It's an important element that could unify the composition and provide a backdrop against which the landscape designer could create contrast, depth, and a sense of continuity through the ever-changing seasons. We're speaking, of course, about stones and their proper grouping.

Stones by their very nature are the perfect complement to bedding plants. They are immutable, remaining as solid, unmoving features of the landscape, whereas plants will grow, bloom, and fade according to the whims of nature; they are hard by nature, existing as strong and durable monuments, while plants are soft, bending and swaying with every passing breeze or rain shower; and, unlike plants, they require no maintenance. A well-designed stone grouping provides a focal point and a setting that shows off a planting design — a stage upon which to play out the drama of colors and textures provided by the designer's plant choices. In addition, stone groupings can be used as a reflection of the local geology and landforms. They create a subtle relationship with the surrounding environment that would be missing in a landscape made up solely of plantings.

Plants and stones are natural partners.

The use of stones in the landscape is growing as people see the dramatic improvement it can make in the overall composition of their planting arrangements. However, landscaping with stones is not as easy as simply plunking down some rocks into the middle of a group of plants. Many design considerations go into creating a pleasing stonescape, such as integrating and balancing the hardscape of stone with the softscape of plants, and placing the stones with an eye to both how they work together as a group and how they fit into their environment. We use nature as our inspiration for the principles of design as well as the layout of stone compositions, mimicking the formations and

relationships found in nature. Natural stonescapes can be modeled after mountains, rivers, waterfalls, peninsulas, lake shores, cliffs, ravines — any geological formation you can think of — and, once placed in the garden, can bring the same sense of grandeur, wonder, and peacefulness to the garden that you might have felt as you first glimpsed any of the natural wonders present in the world around us.

Used well, stone complements and enhances every landscape. With this book, we hope to teach garden enthusiasts and landscape designers alike about the fine art of stone placement as well as some of its practical aspects: where and how to find stone, how to work with stone, and how to pick out just the right stones for a project. Whether you already have a beautifully designed landscape or are starting fresh, we hope that you will find this both an inspiring argument for and an informative guide to creating and building natural stonescapes.

The natural geological formations that surround us provide an endless supply of inspiration for stone compositions. This mountain range along the Li River in Guilin, China, inspired early Chinese artists whose work later influenced the evolution of Japanese garden designers who, in turn, provide a foundation of knowledge and design principles for stonescapes around the world today.

Fascination with Stone

I believe in the activity of stone, actual or illusory. . . . They say in Japan that the end interest of old men is stone — just stone, natural stone, ready-made sculptures for the eyes of connoisseurs. This is not quite correct, it is the point of view that sanctifies; it is selection and placement that will make of anything a sculpture. . . .

— Isamu Noguchi
A Sculptor's World

Since the beginning of recorded history, and probably before, there has been a special relationship between people and stone. This fascination has expressed itself in a variety of ways, but the cultural and historical expressions are among the most revealing. Ancient cultures used stone as a building element because of its durability and permanence in the landscape; indeed, many of these sturdy artifacts from our distant past are with us today. Witness the aqueducts and the Coliseum of Rome, the pyramids and Sphinx of Egypt, and Greece's Parthenon. In addition, stone was used in many of the more intimate and intriguing landscapes in history.

Easter Island

Many people are familiar with the giant stone heads on Easter Island. Some of these stones are over 60 feet (18 m) in height (equivalent to a five-story building) and 300 tons (272,400 kg) in weight. The purpose of these mysterious figures is a riddle to this day. Some believe that an obsessive cultural behavior resulted in the frenetic creation and celebration of these icons of stone.

◄ Across the length and breadth of Easter Island, hundreds of mysterious giant stone figures stand guard.

T'ai Hua Stones

In China is found a particular type of limestone that has been deeply pitted and eroded by the actions of water over a long period of time. In a landscape, these unique, convoluted stones can take on a quality of lightness and delicacy not unlike clouds. They are highly revered; in particular, those that originate from T'ai Hua Lake are quite valuable. At one time the entire treasury of China was bankrupted by the passion of the Emperor Hui-tsung (A.D. 1100–1126) for these stones.

Stonehenge

Over four thousand years old, the famous stone circle commonly known as Stonehenge is only one of many such monuments that dot the English countryside. An extraordinary amount of time and effort were expended to create this massive structure: The stones had to be quarried and then hauled many miles to reach their final resting site, all without the benefit of cranes, wheels, or other labor-saving devices. Few of the other stone circles throughout the British Isles have the significance of Stonehenge. Still, their sheer profusion is testimony to the importance of stone in the cultural landscapes of England, Ireland, and Scotland.

T'ai Hua stones make unique focal points.

Stonehenge is thought to be an astronomical reckoning system that was used to track celestial events such as solstices and eclipses.

Stone upon stone, the *menhirs* march like soldiers in formation across the ancient landscape of Carnac.

Carnac

There are also standing stones in the landscapes of France and other European locations. Here, however, they're commonly colonnades of stones, which sometimes stretch for miles. The *menhirs* (upright stones) of Carnac in Brittany, France, constitute the largest array of these colonnades in the world, and predate Stonehenge by nearly two thousand years. At Le Ménec, a small village in Carnac, 1,099 stones stand in 11 separate corridors that stretch to the horizon. At one end of the arrangement, the stones are close to 12 feet (3.7 m) in height; at the other end they diminish to 3 feet (.9 m) in height. At one complex, the largest stone (*Er Grah,* or "The Fairy Stone") stood 65 feet (20 m) tall and weighed close to 350 tons (317,800 kg). Unfortunately, an earthquake toppled this stone in 1722.

STONEWORK IN JAPAN

Stone plays a significant role in the built landscape of Japan. The enthusiastic use of stone can be traced to a reverence for nature reflected in Shinto, a religion rooted in traditional Japanese culture and practiced by many to this day. The Shinto faith incorporates the concept of animism, the belief that spirits dwell in natural objects such as stones, so stones were especially meaningful garden elements.

Japanese gardens are considered to be among the most beautiful and tranquil gardens in the world. Nature is the model for the Japanese garden, so inevitably stones often take center stage in these peaceful spaces. Indeed, you can find numerous examples of stones as both cultural and natural artifacts in Japanese gardens of all types. Entire "nurseries" in Japan are dedicated to supplying decorative stones and cultural artifacts constructed of stone; most garden centers devote a separate section to stone artifacts and stones for use as garden objects. Japanese gardens have become famous for the myriad stonescapes they employ.

Bonsai

The planting of miniature trees in shallow dishes is an art form known popularly as bonsai, and it is a favorite activity of many gardeners around the world. In essence, the creator of this natural tableau seeks to duplicate in the viewer the feeling derived from nature through the artful manipulation and placement of both living and nonliving objects. Bonsai designers often incorporate small stones into these compositions in a way that gives the stones a meaningful relationship with the tree or trees. Two common styles are roots-over-rock and clinging-to-a-rock, which mimic scenes often seen in mountainous or rocky areas. Roots-over-rock is common along rocky streams whose shores have been eroded by seasonal flooding. A mature tree's roots will have grown over stones buried in the soil; when the earth is washed away during floods, the boulder that remains still has the roots clambering over its surface. Clinging-to-a-rock is typically found where snow, ice, or avalanche has eroded cliffs and mountainsides, shearing away tons of stone and leaving behind the exposed roots of a tree above.

The patient gardener can duplicate the natural phenomenon of roots-over-rock, as shown in this woodland site in southern Ohio, by covering the stone with soil, planting the miniature tree, and then slowly removing the soil.

Raked-Gravel Gardens

The so-called Zen meditation gardens — stones surrounded by raked gravel — are a form of gardening known in Japan as *Karesansui*, or "Dry Landscape." A well-designed garden of this type can show all of the classic elements of a landscape, including depth, balance, contrast, movement, and rhythm. Many of the original dry gardens were rife with symbolism and myth. The most common designs incorporated traditional metaphors for longevity and immortality — important cultural themes in Japan. Another common approach to designing these gardens was to mimic the natural landscapes of distant places.

This raked-gravel garden in Portland, Oregon, dramatizes with one scene the story of the Buddha who allowed himself to be eaten by seven starving tiger cubs, thus revealing the compassion of the Buddha for all forms of life. Although set on a still and silent stage of sand and rock, the viewer has an impression of great energy and tension.

Suiseki

In Japanese *suiseki,* the artist finds stones reminiscent of various natural forms and displays them in containers chosen to show off their inherent beauty (often wooden platforms). The intention is to capture the natural rhythm and structure of unique natural formations and mountain ranges, and thus give the viewer the same emotional response evoked by the larger original. *Suiseki* can evoke memories in viewers of distant places they have visited, of other landscapes in other times. The memories of towering stone monoliths, cold mountain streams, and cascading waterfalls refresh and energize whoever stops to look and see that which lies deeper than the surface.

Cultural Artifacts

Because of its convenience and durability, stone was the medium of choice for creating functional and aesthetic articles for everyday use in ancient Japan. These articles are still crafted and used today, not only in rural areas but also in formal gardens. The list of stone artifacts in the Japanese garden includes such diverse items as lanterns, pagodas, wash basins, pathways, wells, and troughs. You can even find what could best be described as the Japanese equivalent of the American pink flamingo — whimsical carved stone cats and stone badgers decorating the entry gardens of Japanese homes.

In this example of *suiseki,* the viewing stone is set on a simple unadorned platform, inviting viewers to focus on its natural inherent beauty.

MOVING STONES IN MODERN TIMES

The penchant for using stones in our private and public gardens continues to this day and shows every sign of increasing in popularity. Drive around a residential neighborhood or through a mall or shopping center; evidence of stones in the built landscape will be readily apparent. Some of our enthusiasm for rocks can be traced to just before the turn of the century: The gardeners of the Victorian era sought to create ornate and formal balance in the landscape, but in an informal and naturalistic style reminiscent of the Japanese approach. These gardens celebrated nature, and they often held placed stones.

Collin's Circle

In Portland, Oregon, Robert K. Murase, FASLA, designed an outstanding stone landscape as part of a 100-foot (31 m) wide traffic circle. Close to 80 percent of its surface is filled with huge basaltic boulders, a few of which stand upright. The inspiration for Collin's Circle is the

Collin's Circle, by Robert Murase, is a good example of stone placement whose inspiration is both naturally and culturally derived.

geology of lava flows in central Oregon, but Murase also attributes a good deal of his design to the stone circles of England. Murase is well known for his masterful use of stones in the landscape and is highly regarded for his work on the haiku-inspired Japanese-American Plaza piece *Talking Stones*.

Ascension

Rick Anderson of South Carolina is a landscape artist whose passion for stones is evident in nearly all of his work. The first clue is the name of his company — Stōn Wûrks. His work with stones includes stone walls and walkways but also ventures into realistic dry streams, wet waterfalls, and whimsical concoctions fresh out of his fertile imagination.

One of the more ambitious projects he coordinated was the installation of over 270 tons (245,160 kg) of stones in a piece that he describes as a "metaphor for a waterfall." Called *Ascension*, it is located at a major entry point into the city of Columbia, South Carolina, and is composed of two types of stone. One type is an earth-colored schist, and it makes up the basic structure of the rocks that form a waterfall. The other, milky quartz, implies the foaming waters cascading through the stones. Although the composition is dramatic during the day, it's at its best at night: The lights reflect off the milky quartz and, as you drive by, the falls actually seem to move.

The dynamic of dark and light stone in Ascension, by Rick Anderson, uniquely captures a sense of implied movement.

River Stacks

In the town of Williamsburg, Massachusetts, an anonymous landscape artist stacks stones in the Westfield River. He takes the rounded and erratic stones he finds in the depths of the river and along its banks and stacks them in columns of various heights and shapes. The work is very temporary — when the river rises and swifter currents prevail, the carefully placed stone arrangements are swept away or broken apart. He says, "I find myself rediscovering stones I have used over and over again. It's like old familiar friends whose faces are intimately known." The locations and shapes of the stacked stones are constantly in flux, so they are more in tune with the impermanence of nature than with the implied finality of most works of humankind.

Rooftop Stonescape

Capturing the Maine forest atop a roof was no small feat. We employed a crane to lift much of the stone —the giant artificial stone can be seen in the lower right-hand corner.

On the low rooftop of WCSH television in downtown Portland, Maine, we collaborated on a unique rooftop stonescape. Our design intent was to capture a natural scene representative of Maine's rugged geography, so we used not only plant materials but also the stones so much in evidence throughout the state. We lowered several pieces of

stone onto the roof with a crane, then assembled them to represent an eroding knoll. One difficulty we encountered was that from a design perspective, it was important that we place a massive angular boulder on one end of the garden — to frame the composition as well as lead the eye into the grouping. But it was a relatively small roof, and we had to consider the weight of such a stone; also, for lack of soil we couldn't bury it more than 12 inches (30 cm). In order to meet these criteria, we chose an artificial stone that had the appropriate angle and mass to fill our design's needs.

The backdrop cliff of this zooscape is constructed entirely of artificial stone. Taking into consideration the natural effects of weathering on stone found in nature, diGiacomo fabricated the black horizontal lines as a representation of the eroded streaks of soft quartz often found in actual granite formations.

diGiacomo, Inc.

One of the foremost commercial artisans of stone placement is diGiacomo, Inc., a landscape design company based in Azusa, California. It is best known for creating geologically and geomorphically correct artificial rock formations and water features around the world. By combining a knowledge of geology and art, diGiacomo creates stunning works of artificial stone that evoke powerful feelings in the viewer. Designing with real rocks is a natural extension of their work; one example can be found at the Fog Garden of Harvard University, for which they selected and placed the stones. Other current projects and works-in-progress include stone compositions for Oakley's corporate headquarters, the interior of Timberland Shoe stores, the Donald Trump International Golf Club in West Palm Beach, Florida, as well as the flagship store of L.L. Bean in Freeport, Maine.

Masahiko Seko

A landscape designer who recently moved from Inazawa, Japan, to the United States, Masahiko Seko brings with him a time-honored tradition of working with stones in the landscape. He says, "Always be looking around at nature because it tells us what to do when we design the landscape. To make stones look more natural in the landscape, we need to understand how they work in nature." His work reflects that understanding. Although Masahiko can and does build authentic Japanese gardens, he also creates Western compositions that are uniquely contextual to each site and bioregion. He applies the depth of design knowledge he gained in Japan to each client's space; his use of stones is masterful and cosmopolitan.

Masahiko Seko borrows heavily from nature as well as Japanese tradition to create stunning works of art.

Murmuring Flow

In southwestern Connecticut, a 450-foot (137 m) long stone sculpture runs through a walled garden, past a terrace, and into a clearing in a wood. This monumental work is by Janis Hall, well recognized for her reverence for and use of natural materials and forms in built landscapes. In many respects it is a celebration of the numerous rocky streams found in the area. One of the most striking aspects of this stone placement is Hall's ability to capture the rhythm and cadence of a natural stream. Although water does not actually flow through the "stream," you can almost hear the murmuring sounds of imaginary waters. By understanding and applying the lessons of the land that is close at hand, Hall fit her composition to its bioregional context. This gives the work meaning and a sense of place within the landscape.

Janis Hall's representation of the energy of the dry stream parallels the energy of the adjacent walkway, reinforcing the feeling of movement.

Stone's Role in the Landscape

2

A friend once told us that she thought the garden was an improvement on nature. While this is an arguable point, the underlying implication is that we find inspiration for gardens in the natural world. The improvements we then bring to the designed landscape include control over what blooms and when; control over the way in which certain views are framed; and a certain control over the order of elements, and their relationship to each other. What is interesting is that although we rely on nature as a resource in planning and fleshing out our gardens, we rarely take the time to think of all of the bounty that the natural world has to offer. Specifically, geology is part of our natural world, and we should remember it when we design our landscapes. Using stones helps make our gardens fuller pictures of the natural world. In other words, well-placed stones in the landscape can make that landscape more complete.

A QUIET VOICE

When properly and consciously set in a landscape, stones become the voice of the designer. They speak to the viewers about the garden — its layout, its boundaries, its purpose, the relationships among its elements, and its inspiration. You can plan and manipulate the way in which you place the stones to direct, influence, or inspire the viewer's perspective of and emotional response to the landscape. Although there are a number

◀ Natural stonescapes come in all shapes and sizes, with a never-ending variety of plantings and preexisting site amenities. A stonescape's most important purpose is to enhance the sense of nature at work by providing continuity of texture and form among all the different elements of any given landscape.

of design considerations to be dealt with in their placement, the most important purposes of stones in the landscape are:

- To serve as focal point
- To frame a focal point or particular view
- To provide textural contrast
- To direct eye movement
- To build a sense of depth
- To fit the landscape to its bioregional context

Focal Point

A *focal point* is a place that you, as designer, want to draw particular attention to. Stones can be a dramatic way of accomplishing this. By adding even a single stone that has unique features, you can give a spot in your garden a greater sense of character, and enhance the visitor's satisfaction. It is best to contrast the relative lightness or darkness of a focal-point stone against its opposite. By using a dark evergreen behind a light-colored stone, for instance, you will allow the stone to stand out more and better fulfill its role as a focal point.

This unusual stone looks like a head canted to one side. Its orange-red color contrasts greatly with the green behind, dramatically enhancing its use as a focal point in the garden.

Framing

Framing helps create a fuller and better-defined picture. A painting or a photograph that is matted and framed is more aesthetically appealing by far than its unframed counterpart. A frame is generally made up of horizontal and vertical lines that contain the view of a particular area, and stones or a stonescape can make beautiful and unusual framing lines. Try using stones to frame the view of a focal-point stone: Frame the front or bottom of the viewed space with a stone wall or path, for example, or use an overhanging rock to mark the side or top of the space. The resulting image will be very powerful. Framing lines can also be tree branches, fences, sidewalks, roof lines, overhanging rocks — just about anything that marks the edge of the viewed space.

Directing Eye Movement

Use stones to guide a visitor's eye through the landscape by pointing it in a particular direction. For example, the angle of the stones in the ground can lead the eye to a particular point that you want the visitor to see. Also, if stones are repeated along a certain line on the ground and get either larger or smaller, the eye of the visitor will tend to follow their progress.

The vertical stone on the right nicely frames this carefully cultivated landscape and mirrors the tall tree on the left, which frames the other edge of the landscape — defining and containing a square perspective.

Stone provides an enlivening contrast to the texture and color of the dense, shrubby bush and the more delicate ferns, increasing the sense of energy and life exuded by the multicolored pebbles of this path.

Contrast

Contrast can bring a garden to life. Use stone in your garden to contrast with the plants that surround it. These can include not only typical garden plants but also the trunks or leaves of trees and the foliage of shrubs or their fruit. The textures and shapes of stones can provide a wonderful contrasting backdrop for seasonal blooms.

Depth

Adding depth can make a landscape look larger than it is. By establishing a foreground, a middle ground, and a background, you let the visitor know where the front and back of your composition are. This feeling of containment or groundedness transmits a sense of tranquillity and peacefulness to the viewer. Stones can be the perfect tool for establishing foreground or midground. (See page 46 for a discussion on creating and manipulating depth in a stonescape.)

The two stones in this backyard composition establish the foreground ▶ of the view, containing the site and providing a sense of depth.

In this arrangement, carefully designed for bioregional context, the stones are of the same light, chalky texture found on cobbles and mountaintops, and the layout of stones and shrubby evergreens mimic the shape of the mountaintop in the distance.

Bioregional Context

By creating stone groupings that are true to the nature of the geology they exist in, you better define the location of your garden. A *bioregion* is an area of land whose flora, fauna, geology, and meteorology are contained within a natural boundary, such as the largest watershed in the area. To better understand how to use stones in the context of your bioregion, go out and explore rock outcroppings and ledge formations within a short driving radius of where you'll build your garden.

BUILDING RELATIONSHIPS WITH PLANTS

One of the most basic tenets of using stones in the garden is that they should work effectively with the garden's plantings. Although there are gardens in which stone is the only element, such as the raked-gravel, or Zen meditation, gardens of Japan (see page 5), they are more the exception than the rule, and such gardens do not usually fit with the cultural context of most homes. While they are beautiful, and can effectively use all of the design rules and considerations we will discuss in the following pages, they do not typify the use of stones in the vast majority of home, municipal, or corporate landscapes. Using plants in connection with stones is by far the norm, so you should consider the relationship of stones to plants part of the rules of behavior for using stones in the garden.

It's important to recognize that the plants and stones together will have a working, dynamic relationship. There are four basic considerations for making this relationship a success: backdrop, space definition, diversity, and substitution.

The simplest rule in placing plants together with stones is that you should place the plants close enough to the stones that, as they establish themselves, they will grow to completely surround the stones.

Backdrop

A dramatic way to use stones in the garden is to display colors and textures against their surfaces. A common problem in garden design is that the more dramatic textures and colors become lost in a profusion of plantings. To address this, dark evergreens are often used as background for light-colored foliage, or dark or richly colored flowers and plants are contrasted against bright or light-colored flowers and plants. The same idea applies to stones. Since they can be dark, neutral, or light in color, stones are excellent foils against which to display plantings. In some cases you may even want to drape the foliage of a particularly interesting plant over the top of a stone to show off its color and texture to the utmost. A fine-textured threadleaf Japanese maple, for example, will dramatically show its beautiful texture when displayed against a stone.

Space Definition

One of the factors that helps us appreciate a space aesthetically is a clear definition of what is going on within it. You can use stones to clearly define specific areas within your garden. In a well-designed grouping, individual stones will seem part of a single whole. Plants that you associate with this grouping will become part of that whole. The plant choices you make will help set off the stone grouping, and the stone composition will help define the planting area — it's a win-win situation. By defining the space of the garden, the stones can provide depth, unity, and focus to an otherwise unruly gathering of plants.

The dark and muted expanse of stone in this stonescape provides a wonderful backdrop for the brilliant colors and fine texture of these plantings.

Diversity

Diversity of elements in a landscape is a powerful tool for creating a "natural" atmosphere. Rarely will you find a uniform row of flowers or plantings growing wild in field or forest. An effective way to mix stones with plantings is to use them to break up a mass planting of a single-textured plant. Junipers, daylilies, many ground covers, and certain annual bedding plants fall into this category. A single-textured ground cover can be uninteresting or even boring. Stone, however, can act as a focal point that brings diversity and helps lend a certain meaning or definition to the space. For example, if you place multiple stones of the same geological origin in a mass of plantings or ground cover, a composition will begin to take shape that seems far more encompassing than the individual rocks themselves. The ground cover will appear to cover the hidden parts of a much larger geological formation.

The low-lying horizontal stone in the foreground helps to break up and balance an unruly mass of plantings. Notice how the overlay of plants on top of and around the stone gives the impression that the stone forms part of a greater underlying geological formation.

A single stone catches the wind, gathering snow into an ever-shifting sculpture.

Substitution

Unfortunately, in many parts of the world we are without herbaceous plants in the wintertime. Flowers and foliage disappear, and we are without their colorful presence for many months, left anxious for their return. The advantage of using stones in colder climates, then, is that they stay throughout the year. If you create a well-thought-out stone arrangement, you can provide a welcome visual relief in the seasonal absence of those plantings. In some cases, people create stone arrangements that are totally hidden from view during the growing season, leaving the stone for "eye candy" during the bleak months of winter.

In the parts of the world that receive snow, stone compositions can also create dramatic miniature landscapes through the winter. When the wind blows snow into drifts, the underlying ground forms and extrusions affect the shape the snow takes as it settles. The beautiful windblown sculptures that drifting snow forms atop rocks take on an ephemeral quality that cannot be duplicated.

Examining the Site

3

There is a great deal to think about when you first go about placing stones into your landscape, whether as groupings or individual accent stones. In fact, it's often surprising just how much there is to think about when designing any space, regardless of the medium. Some of the major factors influencing stone placement are determined by the site you are working with: its constraints, perspectives, and obfuscating elements, as well as any preexisting elements or structures that could be used to frame views or create a sense of depth. Any one of these can complement or detract from your composition, so before any discussion of stone selection, where to find stones, or how to put them into the ground, it is essential that you, the prospective designer, be well grounded in these important factors.

A thorough understanding of basic design principles and how they apply to stones in the landscape will greatly enhance your chances of picking the right stones for your project and site. For example, if you understand depth and scale, you will have a better idea of what size of stones you will need to complement the space that you are designing. This will save valuable hours at the quarry and allow you to focus on other aspects of your design. The basic design principles discussed in this and the next chapter will help you to rough out a plan for your stonescape and determine, if you don't already have them on-site, what type of stones you'll need and how many you should collect. Whether you are experienced or just beginning to learn about stonescaping, following a checklist of design considerations will not only save you some time and money, but may also evoke thoughtful and creative insights that will help you to draft the plan for your composition.

Design Considerations

I. Reviewing Site Constraints
  A. Relative Malleability
  B. Soil Conditions
  C. Legal Restrictions
  D. Rights-of-Way
  E. Access

II. Examining Point of View
  A. Primary Point of View
  B. Secondary Point of View
  C. Tertiary Point of View

III. Avoiding Obfuscation
  A. Obstructions
  B. Lines
    1. Tangential Lines
    2. Crossing Lines
    3. Lines of Redirection
  C. Shadows
  D. Distractions
  E. Texture and Contrast

IV. Framing
  A. Horizontal Elements
  B. Vertical Elements
  C. Diagonal Elements
  D. Positioning within the Frame

V. Creating Depth
  A. The Grounds
  B. Defined Edges
  C. Reflection
  D. False Perspective
  E. Site-Specific Depth Creation
    1. Large Stones in a Small Space
    2. Small Stones in a Large Space
    3. Large Stones in a Large Space
    4. Small Stones in a Small Space
    5. A Deep and Wide Site
    6. A Shallow and Wide Site
    7. A Shallow and Narrow Site
    8. A Deep and Narrow Site

VI. Context and Motivation
  A. Internal Context
    1. Lines of Force
    2. Repetition of Lines and Forms
    3. Implied Planes
    4. Dynamic Spacing
    5. Plantings
  B. External Context
    1. Movement
    2. Architectural Elements
    3. Plantings
  C. Bioregional Context

VII. Working with Ratios
  A. Vertical to Vertical Ratios
  B. Horizontal to Horizontal Ratios

VIII. Creating Rhythm, Style, and Emphasis

IX. Maintaining Balance
  A. Formal Balance
  B. Informal Balance

X. Reviewing Scale
  A. Relative to the Site
  B. Relative to People

XI. Creating Illusions
  A. Making a Small Space Look Large
  B. Making a Large Space Look Small
  C. Distortions

XII. Designing around Site Amenities
  A. Walks
  B. Patio
  C. Walls
    1. Retaining Walls
    2. Freestanding Walls

CREATING A PLAN
FOR A STONE COMPOSITION

When designing a garden plan, landscape professionals usually draft a preliminary design on paper or computer. Stone, however, is an entirely different matter. Why? Well, first, you won't always know the size, texture, or color of the stones you'll be using for your composition; second, subtleties of the site will determine exactly the best way to place the stones in the soil; and finally, the way in which you can consider using the particular character of your stones and site will be effected by the purpose or function of the space being designed. Once you're on-site with stones, the execution of a design drafted on paper can be interpreted in as many different ways as there are people to read that design. The process of creating a plan for a stone composition is most often a hands-on experience. Although you can study your stones and site and create a rough working plan, such as those shown in chapter 8, you must be prepared to be flexible and allow your plan to change and accommodate the subtleties of stones and site as you progress through the placing of the stones.

Before you begin to rough out a plan, there are four primary considerations that you will want to examine:

- **Site.** The site's size, topography, and points of view will influence the scale and placement of the composition.
- **Stone.** The stone's character and physical appearance will influence the internal dynamics of the composition.
- **Purpose.** The intended purpose of the space will effect the lines of force that influence the movement and direction of the inherent energy of the stone grouping.
- **Bioregional context.** The bioregion that you're working in will provide a context of surrounding geology and environment for your design.

The advanced and/or experienced designer of stone groupings will find that these influences can be dealt with on an intuitive level. What would be most helpful for you is to quickly check over the list of design considerations at left to make sure that your composition realizes its full potential.

A beginner just starting down the road of planning a stone composition, however, may do best to proceed step-by-step through a plan, examining each of the design considerations in turn, as outlined and discussed in this and the next chapter.

(For further discussion of designing a plan, see Marking the Layout on page 99.)

REVIEWING SITE CONSTRAINTS

One very important design consideration is the extent of site constraints that you will need to deal with. They can include the relative malleability of your soil, soil conditions, legal restrictions, rights-of-way, and, especially, your access to the site.

Relative Malleability

How deep can you dig? Where is the water table? Will you affect any nearby wells if you excavate below a certain level? What type of soil are you working with as a base? You should find answers to these types of questions early on, because they will have a large influence on what direction your design can take. Good resources include state cooperative extension services, state geological services, or the local town or city administration.

Soil Conditions

In order to know how to set your stones in the earth, you need to know if there are any precautions you need to take to ensure that the earth does not later unsettle your stones. If you're working in the North in a wet or flood-prone area, or if the soil you're working with doesn't drain well, you may want to consider instituting drainage beneath your larger stones. If you live in an area of landfill reclaim or new construction, you may need to compact the earth around your stones to keep it from tipping over as the earth settles beneath it.

Legal Restrictions

Landscaping legalities vary from community to community and require some research on your part. Zoning laws and setback requirements can be an issue — check in with the zoning board of appeals for your town or city. You need to educate yourself on what you can and cannot do around your home or the home you are working on. If you feel you need to contest city ordinances on this issue, don't despair — it's not impossible. Although it may mean taking a couple of evenings out of your life, you can always plead your case to the zoning board of appeals in the community you're working in. Be prepared to explain why this property should be granted a variance. We highly recommend that you talk to all of the people that surround the property, as well. Tell them about your intentions, your design, and how you think it will benefit the landscape.

Rights-of-Way

Rights-of-way can effectively restrict you as well. If a utility company has a right-of-way through your property, it has the right to come back at any time in the future and tear up whatever is in the way (provided it is in response to an emergency or part of regular maintenance). Also think about public rights-of-way. Imagine you have a cabin on the shore of a lake. In the summer, beachgoers will show up and want to access the lake. If you have placed your stone grouping in the right-of-way these people need to get to the lake, they may go right through it. They have the right to do so, and you could find yourself in the middle of a losing legal battle. To avoid this type of problem, find out in advance from the county tax maps where public-access rights-of-way are.

Access

It is especially important to consider how accessible the site is to you and the equipment available to you. In Japan, lack of access often makes it next to impossible for any heavy equipment to work in backyards. In some such cases, designers employ cranes to deliver large stones and even huge plant material by lifting them right over the house.

Before designing for a space, review chapter 6 and/or talk to your contractors to find out the space requirements of each piece of equipment you'll need. Also, make a special visit to the site to understand exactly what your limits will be. This visit will strongly influence your design. At times, successful delivery and placement may require cooperation from an adjacent landowner. If you (or your client) and the neighbor are not on good terms, and chances are slim that you will be able to use that neighbor's property for access with trucks and equipment, this could influence your selection of materials and the type of design you create. On the other hand, if there are no bad feelings, you may be able to persuade the neighbor to grant access by expounding upon the beauties of a good stonescape and how it may be profitable as well (by enriching the view or even raising average property values in the neighborhood).

Working with a Malleable Landscape

If you are fortunate enough to have a great deal of flexibility in how far down you can dig and how high you can build, use it! People respond very positively to vertical compositions, so dig down deep to set tall stones erect in the ground. The landscape does not need to remain a flat plane.

EXAMINING POINT OF VIEW

One important area of design consideration is the point of view (P.O.V.) of the person or people who will be immersed in the landscape, or the views of the composition that will most often be seen. For example, if not planned properly, a group of stones in your backyard may look its best from only one perspective, which may not even be the perspective from which most people will view it — the back door, for instance. From that particular point of view, the composition may come together as a unified whole, but from another point of view, such as the street or bedroom window, it might just look like a bunch of unrelated rocks. The trick lies in designing a grouping that looks good from several different positions. Therefore, try to consider what your composition will look like from at least three points of view: primary, secondary, and tertiary.

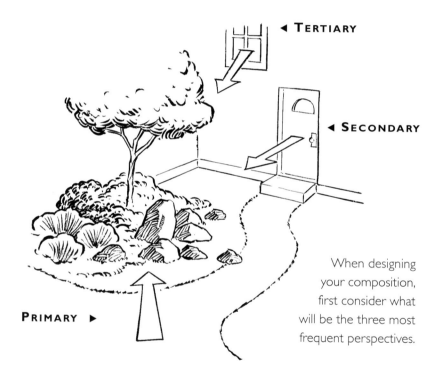

When designing your composition, first consider what will be the three most frequent perspectives.

Dual Primary Points of View

In certain situations, you can have two divergent viewpoints of the same stone grouping, each of equal importance. This can be quite a challenge: You will need to arrange the stones to create two separate meaningful forms in the same composition. This situation is typical when you're designing for an entry that is also an exit. When you're walking in one direction the group of stones has one look; seen from the opposite direction it should look like an entirely different, yet whole, composition.

Typical places to look for primary, secondary and tertiary perspectives are entryways and exits, windows, pathways, sitting areas, and stairways. Which area will take precedence? Usually, the normal volume of activity in a given area will determine the primary point of view, although that is not always the case (see the box on page 35). In some circumstances, not only is the *direction* you are looking from important, but so is the *height*. This could be as simple as the difference between sitting on a bench and standing, or it could be the difference between floors in a building. In a contained courtyard of a multilevel apartment complex, there are many points of view, and most of these are on an angle from above.

The differences between sitting and standing are usually subtle, but in one way they can be made quite dramatic: Have an entire stone grouping become apparent *only* when viewed from a single perspective — sitting down. This isolates the experience and can make it more meaningful and powerful to viewers. It becomes a special treat or discovery for the unsuspecting person who happens upon the scene you have created. The art and technique of obscuring the composition from other perspectives vary from site to site. However, whatever artifice you employ, maintaining context and continuity is essential. The manipulation necessary to create the composition should not be apparent; your tools should blend with the rest of the landscape. The simplest way to create such a perspective is when the point of view is from a house window, along a covered walkway, or inside an arbor. You can adjust the physical barriers that frame the view or add new materials, such as cloth, wood, rattan, or bamboo, so that they obstruct the view of the composition from a standing position. When you sit down, however, you would be able to "peek" under the obstruction to see it.

Another powerful yet subtle use of point of view is arranging the stones so that from one perspective only, a face or some other construct appears. If you can create the illusion that all the objects are together in one vertical plane, the textures and lines of the stones will seem to sketch out a desired shape to the viewer. In the real world we see these pictures come together fairly frequently. An obvious example doesn't use stones but something most of us take for granted: our hands and light. Hold your three-dimensional hands up to a bright light and then look at the shadows they cast on the wall; you might see the form of a rabbit or turkey or other fanciful creation. The light merges the three-dimensional elements into a single shape on a vertical plane. The Old Man of the Mountains in New Hampshire is another good example. The profile of a man's head appears against the sky when you view the formation from a certain angle. Other perspectives don't reveal the profile, though, because the alignment isn't quite right.

By understanding exactly where your viewing perspectives will be, you can exercise a certain amount of control over exactly how the observer's eye will be led. You can create subtle or even clearly defined lines and planes within your composition that will help lead the

Profiles or caricatures like the Old Man are quite common in mountainous country throughout the world — it's likely that you have one near your city or town.

eye into and through your composition. For example, you could embed a textured pavement into a walkway that leads the eye from the site of one of the major perspectives to the stone composition. In another example, you could shear plant masses in a way that implies a plane leading across the top of the masses toward the stones. Combining several implied planes whose imaginary intersections join at your stone grouping will pull the eye like a compass needle to magnetic north.

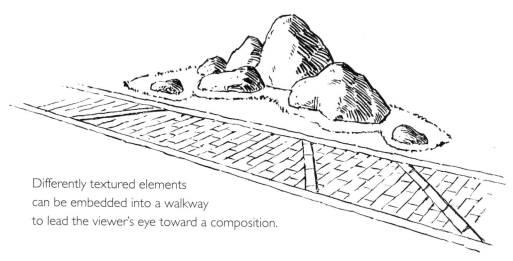

Differently textured elements can be embedded into a walkway to lead the viewer's eye toward a composition.

Primary Point of View

The *primary point of view* is the line of sight that people are most likely to use to view an object or composition. This can vary significantly from situation to situation, but at times you can control exactly where that line of sight is located. For example, you can manipulate the foot-traffic pattern at a built site by changing a door location or the routing of a walkway. You can also create a clearly defined physical or visual destination by leading the eye naturally to rest on your creation (such as by the strategic placement of paths or shearing of bushes described above). The most dramatic way, however, is by creating a specific space whose sole purpose is to contain the stone composition and plantings. Examples include courtyards, walled-in gardens, and pocket gardens. Here you can establish a primary viewing point within the framework of your design with windows, benches, or viewing pavilions.

The largest challenge arises when you have no control over the environment surrounding your stone placements. At this point you need to understand the dynamics of energy and people and how both will flow within any given environment. Within the Eastern culture there are several techniques for choosing perspectives in the placement of objects. If you chose to follow the principles of *feng shui*, the ancient and sophisticated Chinese art and science of placement, you would try to understand the Qi (Chi), the flow of energy in the space, before determining the best location for any feature in the landscape, and especially a stone grouping. The flow of this energy is manifested in nature as wind and water; *feng shui* (which means, literally, "wind and water") can help you understand the imaginary flow of this type of energy in the designed environment. However, *feng shui* principles governing placement aren't always about energy. At times, they arise from Chinese mythology and tradition. In following the tradition of one syle of *feng shui*, a stone grouping would best be placed in the western portion of a space, for instance, because this is the traditional place for metal and stone.

Feng shui is only one of many systems of thought, though. Alternative Eastern or Western philosophies or traditions of placement and composition might indicate other designs. It may be that no one way is necessarily best, or even that you'll have the opportunity to choose. The site, your preferences or those of your client, or the materials at hand may point you toward the appropriate course of action. A good designer will consider all options.

Secondary Point of View

The *secondary point of view* is, obviously, a perspective that does not hold the same importance as the primary P.O.V. However, all of the principles that apply to the primary P.O.V. apply equally to the secondary. It's important to note that this is not a situation where there are two perspectives of equal weight. Unlike the dual primary P.O.V. (see page 30) — two perspectives derived from a common walk where the only variation is direction — the secondary P.O.V. is usually unrelated to the primary perspective in any way.

Tertiary Point of View

The *tertiary* or *third point of view* holds the least relevance of all but should still be considered under certain circumstances. The importance of this perspective comes into play where multiple portals or walkways come together at the stone composition and you as designer have had little control over the existing framework of the contrived space. In these situations, you can at times place additional stones to flesh out and make a complete grouping. These extra stones are usually not visible from either the primary or secondary vantage points. If they do enter into either of these visual images, though, the dynamics of the grouping needs to recognize their presence; in other words, you should establish some relationship between these extra stones and the main grouping, however minor that may be.

A stone composition placed at a juncture of walkways should take on a different form from each of the perspectives.

AVOIDING OBFUSCATION

You must also give careful consideration to various elements in the foreground, middle ground, and background of the viewer's line of sight of the stones. Elements that obscure the perspective of the stone composition, termed obfuscating elements, can include obstructions, tangential lines, crossing lines, lines of redirection, shadows, distractions, and textures and contrast. As a designer, you should consider each of these potential obfuscations in your examination of the site. The conscientious designer looks to the future as well and anticipates problems yet to come. Remember, "yet to come" does not necessarily mean the distant future. It can also mean the difference between daylight and nighttime conditions. If a lamppost will cast evening shadows on your stone composition, you should be aware of this; it will influence the appearance of your work. You do not always have control over factors that change the nature of the site, such as a streetlight shining at night or the seasonal appearance of falling leaves or snow. Still, you should strive to take these factors into account when designing and placing your stone composition.

Obstructions

Anything blocking the view of the composition could be considered an obstruction. It seems fairly obvious that you want to avoid having large objects obstruct lines of sight to your stone placement. But short- and long-term time lines, as well as secondary and tertiary perspectives, are where obstructions will show themselves.

In the short time line, be aware of activities that occur outside the time frame of the design and construction of the grouping. For example, someone might make routine deliveries to the site and stack boxes directly in front of your work; a seasonal activity, such as a harvest festival, could last for an extended time and be set up in the line of sight of the stones; a tenant of the building may regularly park his bright red bicycle in front of the composition. You can deal with this type of obstruction as long as you are aware of the regular pulse of activities that occur on the site, so you can seek out alternative solutions.

In the long-term time line, find out whether any construction or expansion is planned near your site. By talking to the manager of the property or the owner of the house, you can take precautions or even influence their future plans. Another long-term obstruction problem is the growth of existing plants. Future tree or shrub growth may totally envelop a composition, or the rapid expansion of a tall ground cover could hide all of your work very quickly. If you know the growth habits of your plantings and make sure a routine maintenance schedule is put into place, such problems can be "nipped in the bud."

Young plants may seem inconsequential in your stonescape.

However, if left untended, those same plants can grow to swamp and obstruct the view of the composition.

Lines

Any lines suggested by foreign objects (those not a part of your stonescape) can be very distracting. Although they do not directly obstruct the view of the composition, they serve to confuse the eye. Some examples of such lines include planes implied by posts or hedges that are not a part of the designed landscape; the horizontal or diagonal lines of guy wires, clotheslines, or tree or shrub branches; and site amenities such as patios, walkways, or paved surfaces. The position of these lines can have a subtle yet serious influence on the viewer's focus.

Tangential Lines

A *tangent* can be defined as a line or plane that touches another line or plane or an object at just one point. Obfuscating tangential lines are those lines that meet the lines or mass of your composition at a tangent — and for the purposes of this discussion, we can expand this definition to include the *appearance* of touching. This appearance can easily slip by unnoticed because we tend to look and focus first at an object, not its surroundings. For example, imagine taking a picture of your favorite uncle standing in front of the fireplace. When the picture is developed, you discover that Uncle Charlie has sprouted a set of antlers from his head. Of course, actually there was a deer head directly behind him, but the illusion remains because the antlers are at a tangent to Uncle Charlie's head relative to your viewing position. The same principle applies to stones. As with photographs, the usual location of unforeseen tangential lines is in the background of the composition.

The View from the Top

Many designers fail to consider secondary and tertiary perspectives when composing stone placements, so these P.O.V. often suffer obstructions. This is especially true when one of those perspectives is from above. You may find that the canopy of the tree that so nicely provides a high horizontal framing line for the stone grouping from the primary P.O.V. on the ground (a bench in the courtyard, for example) now obscures the vision from the secondary P.O.V. above (a balcony on the second floor, for example). Judicious pruning, moving the composition, or moving the tree may be in order. The best way to avoid these obstruction problems is to be sure to consider those secondary and tertiary perspectives from the beginning.

Crossing Lines

Crossing lines generally lie in the foreground of the composition. They are best classified as obstructions because they stop the eye rather than lead it. When you view your stone grouping through a window, for instance, you may find that the framing elements of each pane of glass tend to cross the composition, which obstructs or misdirects your eye. You can prevent this by removing the small panes of glass and replacing them with a designed window that permits unobstructed views. From secondary and tertiary perspectives, you may find that foreground shrubs or tree branches create crossing lines. Removing the branch may not be the best solution, although it should be considered. You may have better luck, and in fact be able to enhance the composition, by redirecting or training the growth to frame the composition rather than detract from it.

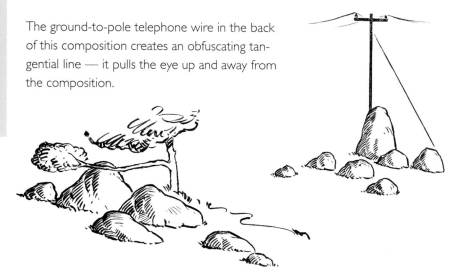

The ground-to-pole telephone wire in the back of this composition creates an obfuscating tangential line — it pulls the eye up and away from the composition.

Sometimes, trees that once complemented a composition will grow branches that become crossing lines, interfering with the viewer's line of sight. If this branch can be trained to grow upward, it will form a nice high horizontal line that will frame the view.

Lines of Redirection

Lines of redirection are usually implied planes (see page 54) or physical lines inside or outside a composition that draw your eye away from the desired center of attention. They could also be implied planes or physical lines that are chaotic — they create no sense of direction whatsoever — and therefore discordant to the composition you are attempting to create. For example, imagine a narrow walkway that runs directly in front of your stone grouping. It does not head into it and does not run perpendicular to it; rather, it runs obliquely from the lower right of your line of sight to the upper left, subtly but powerfully pulling your eye to the left. Solutions for this situation could include masking and hiding the walkway with low shrub masses in the foreground; installing a new walkway that is a mirror reflection of the first walkway, so that the composition sits nestled in the angle between the two lines; eliminating the walkway; and implanting directional lines or implied planes into your landscape that lead the eye to your sculpture, compensating for the walkway's line of redirection.

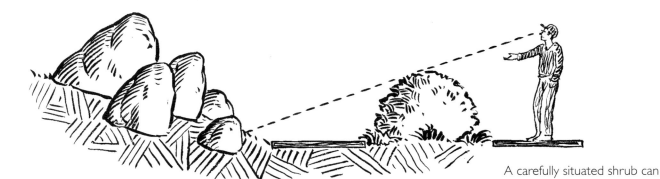

A carefully situated shrub can mask the line of redirection created by a walkway running in front of a grouping.

Shadows

Shadows are obfuscating for the viewer because they redirect the eye, and do not allow the entire composition to be seen with equal weight. They are difficult to judge because they tend to be erratic and to change over both short and long periods of time. Shadows cast at night may be different from those visible in bright sunlight. Also, the sun rises and sets at different times, and its relative height in the sky changes through the seasons, so you have to think in terms of the big picture. You also need to consider the future growth of the trees and other plantings relative to different light sources. Remember these in any follow-up maintenance schedule, too.

You can use shadows to positive effect in your stonescape, but it is unusual and can be difficult. For example, the erratic nature of shadows can help create the illusion of movement in an otherwise static composition. You can also frame a grouping by surrounding it with shadows created by other objects or front-lit stones. This is not to say that the grouping is spotlighted — spotlighting the stones could create deep shadows and contrast that may not be appropriate. With simply natural light playing on the surface of the stones, though, the surrounding shadows serve to frame the stone placement. Shadows can also positively enhance a composition that includes vertical stone masses representing cliffs: Sharp and dark shadows can imply caves or emphasize outcroppings.

Distractions

Distractions are continuous, regular, or periodic situations that draw the viewer's attention away from the desired line of sight. A *continuous distraction* is usually a permanent part of the landscape, such as a sculpture. It might also be a physical destination, such as a bench, or a visual destination, such as a directional or informational sign. The intelligent designer finds a way to obstruct the view of these distractions whenever possible. If you can't hide them, you may need to arrange for their repositioning or removal.

A *regular distraction* is one that occurs on a regular schedule. You might find yourself faced with an irrigation sprinkler timed to come on at a specific time every day, or a flashing sign that comes on between sunset and midnight every night. You should also be aware of human habits that could become a regular distraction, such as someone regularly placing a brightly colored object (car, coat, bicycle, ad infinitum) in a place that would pull the eye from your composition.

A *periodic distraction* is the same as a regular distraction but does not occur on a timed schedule. It is erratic, or perhaps the timing between events is so long as to seem erratic. These types of distractions are the most difficult to account for and deal with. Common examples include seasonal rhythms such as leaf drop, snowfall, spring floods, and bird migrations.

Texture and Contrast

Two final obfuscating elements to be concerned with are texture and contrast. A stone mass can be effectively obscured by its surroundings if the texture of the stone mass is essentially the same as that of its surrounding elements. The stone composition will seem to dissolve into the overall picture.

Contrast works on the same principle but encompasses color and shape. If the landscape you are working in already contains a lot of vertical elements, consider creating a horizontally based stone cluster in your composition in order to provide some visual relief and contrast and to make the composition more distinct from the landscape. In a similar vein, if the stones you are working with are light in color and you place them in gravel that is also light, the lack of contrast will effectively obscure the composition. To help the stones stand out, choose a gravel base that is either lighter or darker than your stones.

Planning the Placement 4

There are many historical and cultural architectural patterns that we could use as the basis for the creation of stone groupings, but we prefer to focus on the inspirations that are provided to us in the natural world. Real-life models, such as mountains, cliffs, lake shores, volcanoes, and other naturally occurring geological formations, serve as templates that help guide us in our creations.

This is not to say, however, that simply because a stone or grouping exists in nature, it should be followed as a guide. Natural stone configurations are not all created equal, and they definitely do not all appeal to our sense of aesthetics. As you begin to view the natural world as your inspiration for creating stone arrangements, you may find some natural formations that do not have a pleasing rhythm and, in fact, create a feeling of discord. By better understanding what appeals to you and by knowing what you respond to positively, you can discover those models in nature that best fit your criteria.

What exactly it is that elicits emotional response is open to debate. Still, although it is difficult to exhaustively identify and define those elements that make us feel good when we look at them, there are many "calculate-able" factors that influence the way we feel within a designed space. *Why* we respond positively is something that is best left to the psychologists and not the landscape designers — although that will not stop us from expressing our opinions.

The three basic maxims of planning aesthetically pleasing stone groupings are:

- **Stability.** Stability is intrinsically linked to creating a sense of "naturalness" in your stone arrangement. Obviously, it is important that whatever you place in the ground be physically stable. However, something can be physically stable and still not appear to be part of the earth. If a stone is resting on top of the ground, it is probably stable, but until it is partially buried it does not look "natural." Outside of some glacial erratics (stones that were deposited by glaciers), our geology is either immersed or embedded in the earth. One of the most common problems of stone placements is that the stones look like they were just recently laid there. Embedding the stones in the ground will not only create a sense of stability but will also help connect the stones to the surrounding environment, forging a link to the local bioregion. Traditional thought says, "Put one-third of the stone in the ground." Reality says otherwise. There are times you need only put a few inches (cm) of a 5-foot (1.5 m) vertical stone in the ground for it to stand. In other situations you must put over two-thirds of a stone underground in order to show its best face or feature.

- **Odd numbers.** By some quirk of the human mind, designs of odd numbers seem to be aesthetically more appealing than those of even numbers. Perhaps because we tend to use an informal balance based on the way nature works, odd numbers of stones are easier to arrange. This odd-number principle is frustratingly illustrated by the task of trying to build an arrangement with four stones. It tends to become formally balanced or to feel out of balance.

- **Internal relationship.** When you find stones in natural surroundings, one of the things that stands out about them is that they all look like they are related to each other in some way. Usually, this is because they are of the same type of stone, or because they were part of a larger mass that has since eroded. Typically, when gardens with stones are designed, little thought is given to such internal relationships; each stone is thought of as wholly unique and separate. While this may work on the rare occasion, it usually just makes the landscape appear disjointed and lacking in focus or theme. To create a relationship among the stones in your arrangement, you need to focus on *internal context* (see discussion on page 52).

The following principles will help the budding or experienced stone placer better understand the myriad ways to expand upon these three maxims. We recommend that as you plan your stonescape, you use the outline on page 26 as a checklist until consideration of each of the design concerns becomes instinctual. Remember, though, that although there are many design considerations regarding the use of stones as objects in the landscape, most of it boils down to common sense and a "good eye." Experience is the best teacher; you may want to adhere to that bit of good advice that states, "Go out and make mistakes as fast as you can."

FRAMING

Well-executed framing can make a poor stone placement look good and a good stone placement look great. A good way to understand the impact of framing is to think of a photograph or painting that is not framed or matted. If you place that objet d'art within a frame and a mat that are contextually related to its subject matter and composition (such as a simple black frame for an Ansel Adams photograph, or a wooden frame with a handmade paper mat for a nature print or pressed flowers), you'll lift its aesthetic appeal to an entirely different level. The horizontal and vertical framing elements contain the scene, and the eye doesn't wander off the edge. Something about that containment and capturing of the scene gives the viewer a better feeling. It may be that we feel this way because of our ancestry. Imagine peering out from inside a cave's opening. Our prehistoric relatives felt more secure when they were surrounded on all sides except the front; they could more easily defend themselves, and more clearly see when anything was attacking.

A landscape photographer will often use trees or other objects as framing elements within the picture itself. This creates a better composition and adds to the feeling of depth in the photo. By understanding where people will view your landscape composition from, you as an aware designer can also use soft- and hardscape elements to frame the view you've created, framing your three-dimensional composition the same way a photographer frames one in two dimensions.

The basic tools for framing a composition are horizontal, vertical, and diagonal depth-creating elements, as well as the relative position of the subject matter being viewed. You can use these elements subtly or blatantly, depending on how natural or formal you intend your composition to be.

The Magic Number

Stone compositions are most dramatic when they are limited to nine or fewer stones. A peculiar thing occurs when you use more than nine stones in an arrangement: The eye and the brain seem to cease counting. However, for some stonescapes you may simply need to use more than nine stones. To keep the composition from appearing too "busy," you can:

- Maintain strong lines of force that move only in one direction.
- Bunch the stones into larger masses composed of smaller stones.
- Group stones by texture and appearance, so that there seems to be several smaller compositions within the larger landscape.

Horizontal Elements

You can use any number of natural or built objects as subtle horizontal framing lines. Examples include tree or shrub branches; implied planes within the stone composition itself; water or waterfalls; walls, dams, and bridges; fences; roof lines; and even overhanging stones. By positioning them in any one of the three grounds (see page 44), or artfully positioning your composition to work with them, you can create an informal horizontal framing structure that, although it powerfully guides the viewer's eye, is not obvious to the viewer's brain.

- As a **foreground** element, situate horizontal frames above or below the viewer's head so that they are visible at least peripherally.
- As a **midground** element, place horizontal framing lines in close proximity to the composition.
- As a **background** element, horizontal frames should lie behind the composition. Be aware of how high your composition will reach — although the vertical elements can and most likely will interrupt the horizontal background lines, those lines should not become tangential to the tops of the vertical elements (see the discussion on page 35).

In a more formal or blatant use of framing, the horizontal and vertical elements would be part of a literal frame constructed around the stone grouping. This formal "box" could be in the foreground, such as a window or door opening, or it could more narrowly focus on the composition itself and simply surround it, such as a composition viewed through the rectangular end of an arbor.

Formal Framing

Here is a well-framed composition using both vertical and horizontal framing elements.

Vertical Elements

As with horizontal elements, you can also employ a number of natural or built objects falling within the grounds as subtle, vertical framing elements. Examples include tree trunks, fissures in stones, upright stones, a cliff face, narrow upright shrubs, flagpoles, building edges, ornamental downspouts, fountains, and falling water. The use of vertical elements for framing is normally limited to the foreground and midground areas, because placing them in the background tends to lead the eye up and out of the composition, especially if they are not contained within a horizontal background element. An interesting aspect of vertical framing elements is that they can still be effective if you use them only on one side of the composition.

Diagonal Elements

Diagonal framing elements can effectively contain a view by breaking the composition into a framed space, isolating it and making it a focal point. This is definitely a nontraditional approach, but it's very effective. Vines, ropes, chains, tree trunks or limbs, poles, falling water, and larger stone masses can all serve as your design tools.

Positioning within the Frame

Objects within a framed view are most often centered within the framing elements, but this is not necessarily the most effective approach. Consider instead the *rule of nines*, in which you position the composition within your frame by breaking the area to be viewed into a square or rectangle of nine blocks. You can place the focal point at any of the intersections of the lines creating those nine blocks or in the center of a block; its final placement will largely be determined by the nature of the work and the visual flow you're establishing within the composition. For instance, if strong diagonal lines lead the eye naturally in a particular direction, place your focal point within a target zone defined by the movement of those diagonal lines.

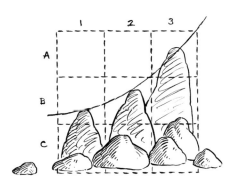

The rule of nines will help you to determine where to place the focal point of a composition; it can also help you to visualize and work with the negative space, as seen in block A-1.

If your site contains strong diagonal framing lines, place the composition or focal point in the target zone defined by the movement of those lines.

CREATING DEPTH

The concept of depth is also critical in the creation of aesthetically appealing stone masses, and it goes hand in hand with good framing. Too much negative space or too much positive space can lead to a very flat or static perspective. By balancing your uses of the space and incorporating depth-creating elements, you will create a harmony that resonates within the dynamics of the designed environment.

Consider the depth of not only the stone mass itself but also the site that contains the grouping. Depth helps define the space of your composition — giving it a front, middle, and back, and locating its edges. Although we may not recognize it consciously, the emotional impact of poorly or well-designed spaces is very powerful (if usually quite subtle). To better understand it, think about dramatic settings and the impact they have on you. If you are walking down a long corridor that becomes increasingly narrower while the ceiling gets lower and lower, you are going to feel an increasing sensation of suffocation and panic. Or walk through a thick fog on a huge flat surface; as you continue to walk with no frame of reference, you'll become increasingly uneasy because you won't know where you are, where you have come from, or where you are going.

Most designed environments are not this dramatic, but the effects, although reduced, are still there. You can thus use depth to evoke a particular emotional response from the viewer. But an even more important use of depth is to define the space of your composition; without this, viewers will be uncomfortable because they have no awareness of beginning or end — of the boundaries of the view. If viewers cannot see where to look, then the work that you've done designing the stonescape will go unnoticed.

The circumstances surrounding depth factors are mutable, and therefore your solutions will vary. However, in order to address any set of circumstances, you must understand the basic tools that a designer uses to manipulate depth: the grounds, defined edges, reflection, and false perspective. By using these tools knowledgeably, a landscape designer can greatly enhance the sense of space in a designed environment — and so evoke a positive emotional response in the viewer.

The Grounds

Grounds refers to the foreground, midground, and background. Used together in the appropriate ratios (see page 57), they can give a sense of depth to the space you are working in. In nearly all cases, the grounds are stacked: From the point of view of the observer, each level is higher than the last. The relative heights of these elements are largely determined by the overall shape and configuration of the site and your desired design.

Defined Edges

Defined edges help clearly delineate spaces. It is generally not appropriate for your design to let a viewer's eye wander into negative space on its edges. The depth you design in your arrangement is intended to define only the designed view, and negative space can introduce elements that disrupt or negate your work in creating depth in the composition. Defined edges help contain the sides of the area in question. In addition, defined edges are more aesthetically pleasing than blurred boundaries, and people generally respond more positively to them. For example, a lawn that gradually merges into other plants is not as appealing as one that comes to a distinct physical edge. A defined edge could be a fence line, a tree branch, a concrete wall — literally anything that says, "The edge of space is *here!*"

Defining Space

Negative space is empty space. *Positive space* is filled space. In a designed landscape, the positive space defines what is the negative space, but rarely the other way around.

Reflection

You can use reflection to give an illusion of depth and space to your stonescape. One of the easiest ways to create reflection is to use water. Still water that reflects the sky above the landscape creates a sense of huge open space, which adds overall depth to the composition. A broad stream or narrow pond that disappears behind a mass of shrubs, stone groupings, walls, or fences gives the illusion of space continuing beyond the view.

Reflection can also be accomplished by mirroring objects relative to each other. In other words, you can use very similar objects or objects that are exact copies of the original. For example, if you use a tall tree as vertical relief in front of a composition and then reflect it by using another tree of the same stature beyond one of the defined edges, it gives the illusion that the land goes on beyond the limits of the landscape, thus creating a sense of depth.

In this composition, the tall tree in the foreground is mirrored by similar trees on the far side of the stone wall that marks the background, creating a greater sense of depth for the otherwise shallow stone grouping.

False Perspective

The principles of perspective teach us that distant objects appear smaller, parallel lines converge, and colors and shapes tend to mute and soften the farther we are from them. Whether you measure in feet or meters, picture a box that is 8 units tall, 8 units wide, and 50 units long, and open on both ends. If it is perfectly rectangular, you know that the distant end you are looking at is the same height as the one you are standing in front of. It appears to be smaller, however, and the lines running along the edges of the box seem to converge at that smaller opening at the end. Now imagine that the box is not perfectly rectangular; instead, the opening at its far end is 12 units high and 12 units wide. This will give you the illusion that the box is shorter in length. Your eye and brain will assume that the far end of the box is of the same dimensions as the end you are standing at, and because the opening at the far end is not quite as small as it would be if it were the same size as your end, the box appears shorter. If you now go to the far (larger) end of the box and look back, your eye will be fooled again. This time, the other (smaller) end will seem to be farther away than the 50 units you know it to be.

You can easily apply this principle to the built or designed landscape. Think of the site as a glorified box whose edges are defined by various hard- and softscape elements. By understanding this, you can control perspective and influence the ways in which viewers perceive this space.

Shakkei

In Japanese garden design, *shakkei*, translated as "borrowed landscape" or "to capture alive that which is beyond," is often used to create depth. The following story describing one technique used to achieve *shakkei* wonderfully illustrates the properties of reflection and false perspective.

There once was a man who had a small garden adjacent to his neighbor's much larger garden. He approached his neighbor and asked if he could offer him a gift of a stone lantern; he added that he wanted to have the honor of placing it in his garden. His neighbor was most appreciative and agreed. The stone lantern that the man presented as a gift was an exact copy of one he had in his own garden, except smaller. When he placed it in his neighbor's garden, he placed it in such a way that it was visible from his own garden. It now served the dual purpose of not only capturing the distant garden and connecting it with his, but also making the "captured" garden look larger and more distant.

Reflection and false perspective make wonderful partners in manipulating the sense of depth in a composition. For example, if you create depth by repeating objects throughout your landscape, but decrease the size of these repeated objects and place them farther back into the composition or landscape, you create an illusion of depth that is surprisingly effective. Due to the nature of perspective, the mind recognizes that objects appear smaller at a distance. When you compound that by making a smaller copy of an object you can physically know the size of (something up close in the foreground) and place that copy at a distance, it makes the distance seem greater.

Site-Specific Depth Creation

Now let's examine some factors that will influence the creation of depth in your chosen site. Keep in mind that the definitions of size for your site are relative to the situation you are working in. A large space could be the Grand Canyon or it could be your backyard. The same holds true for stones. A large stone could be the height of a three-story building or the height of a child, depending upon the scale of the site in which it will be arranged. Similarly, measurements are relative for shallow versus deep (which define the front-to-back space) and narrow versus wide (which define the left-to-right space).

The relative amount of uncontrollable vertical relief in any one of the situations described below can be critical to your success in creating illusions of depth. Indeed, vertical relief is an important card to play when dealing with space; any constraints in its use can be severely challenging.

Technically defined, vertical relief is any rise above or fall below an imaginary horizontal plane. When horizontal or angular lines dominate an area or landscape, vertical relief is any primarily upright element that serves to break up that horizontal or angular flow. For example, if you have a series of low hedges or shrubs that lend a flat, horizontal look to the landscape, you could break up that flat line by introducing a taller vertical shrub, a tree, or a group of upright stones. This will make the landscape more aesthetically appealing and interesting to the eye. Research has shown that people respond to landscapes of strong vertical relief in a very positive way. In fact, it is one of the criteria that the Forest Service uses when completing an aesthetic evaluation of a site, such as a roadside vista rest stop.

Large stones in a small space
In this environment, use a wide range of heights, and position shorter stones toward the direction of the primary and secondary viewpoints.

Vertical stones work well in this situation because you don't have a great deal of space in which to create horizontal lines for the bases of the groupings. Large stones in a small space can mimic huge natural stone formations if they are primarily vertical and if you scatter a few smaller stones in the foreground, like the fragments that often surround those natural formations. Create horizontal balance with shrubs or other plantings.

Small stones in a large space
Use the smaller stones to create the illusion of fissured larger stones that are part of a large geological formation. A good way to add to this illusion is to create vertical relief by building mounds and digging depressions.

Large stones in a large space
Use the negative space to good advantage in this situation. Foreground stone masses should be buried deeply and provide lines of force leading the eye to the major focal points of the composition. Too many stones will only confuse the eye; choose the ones that unify the composition without distracting from it. Lake fronts are often large-space sites, and create an immense background of negative space; balance that with a significant amount of negative space in the foreground, and bury the foreground stones deeply so that they simply lead the eye on toward focal points in the mid- and background.

Small stones in a small space
Use fine-textured, dwarf-type plantings to create a defined space that gives the illusion of a larger environment. Then add the small stones; they will look large in proportion to the composition.

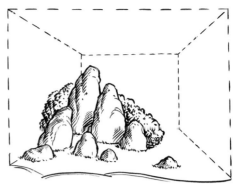

Large vertical stones in a small space can mimic huge natural stone formations.

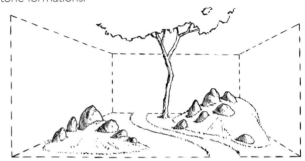

Groupings of small stones in a large space can appear to be the fissured remains of a larger geological formation.

In this large space, foreground negative space balances the background expanse, while large stones lead the eye through the grounds.

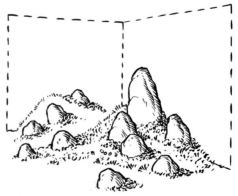

Dwarflike plantings surrounding small stones can create the illusion of a much larger space.

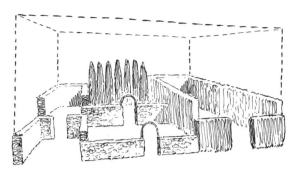

You can also create depth in a deep, wide site by partitioning the space into more manageable, defined "rooms" with fences, shrubs, and trees.

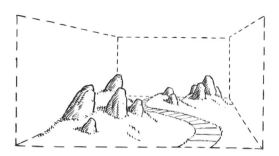

Create a sense of massive space and depth in a deep wide site by mimicking the rolling hills of a natural landscape. Incorporate shrub or tree masses along the edges of the space to imitate the forest boundaries that often mark the end of such spaces.

A deep and wide site

This space should either be partitioned into defined "rooms" or be used in its entirety to mimic rolling hills, meandering rivers or roads, and forest masses in a huge landscape.

A shallow and wide site

This type of site is typically found along a walkway; it affords multiple viewing perspectives that lie obliquely from the direction of traffic flow. The first thing to do is to contain the space with barriers, such as shrubs, fences, or walls. Incorporate trees or other tall elements, such as stones, shrubs, or sculptures, on both sides of the barriers, spacing them to appear random — this "random" spacing will help create rhythm (see page 60) for the composition. These tall elements send a subtle message that the site "goes beyond" the visible space by implying that because you can see them inside as well as outside the defined space, there may be even more farther beyond that you can't see at all.

Then you need to consider how viewers will approach the site (and set up the site to control how viewers approach it) in order to know how and where you will work to create depth.

A. Spread out the grounds obliquely to catch the eye of and lend a feeling of depth to the person who travels through the space on a walkway.

B. Define viewing positions by installing benches, and then set up "vignettes" of depth from those benches.

C. Situate a pergola, or arbor, that would afford various framed-view openings as the person travels the length of the space, and work to create depth in your composition from those lines of sight. You can define the viewpoint even further by setting benches inside the arbor.

D. Exaggerate the vertical relief along the length of the space by using a cliff face or a steep hillside (or a structure that mimics those vertical landscapes, such as the side of a house, as described in the box on page 50). This implies great space beyond.

A. The foreground, midground, and background of this composition are spread obliquely across the shallow, wide site to create a sense of depth.

B. Small "vignettes" of depth can be created in a shallow, wide site for the specific viewing perspectives from benches

C. To further define the viewing perspectives of this shallow, wide site, you can situate benches on the far side of each of the sections of this view-framing arbor.

D. A structure that imitates a cliff or steep hillside, such as this wall, can be used to exaggerate the vertical relief of a composition in a shallow, wide site, helping to create a sense of depth.

Building a "Cliff" in Your Backyard

In the built environment, you can think of the side of a house as the same as the mass of a cliff or steep hillside. By mimicking the characteristics that define a typical cliff face, you can emulate that landscape when designing your garden space. For instance, in one common cliff formation, *slump blocks* lie at the foot of the cliff mass. These are sections that have fallen away from that cliff due to erosion. Travelers usually take a path between the slump blocks and the cliff face. To emulate this landscape with the side of a house, create a slump block from a stone, massed vegetation, or even architectural forms such as sheds or other outbuildings. Just like an actual cliff face, a building that mimics a cliff face exaggerates vertical relief and can create the impression of great space beyond. It's an interesting way to use the objects that occupy space to create the impression of greater space.

The designer of this stone composition cleverly situated a path between two sets of "slump blocks" next to the vertical edge of the side of the house. The meandering of the path out of sight enhances the sense of great space created by this mimicry of a cliff face.

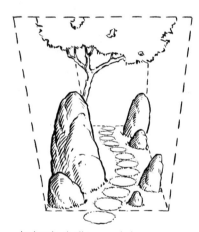

In both shallow and deep narrow sites, use vertical stones along a path to create a sense of entry and journey.

A shallow and narrow site

This type of site needs to be tightly framed. It's unlikely to offer multiple viewing perspectives, so you can focus your attention on a single point of view. Stonescapes in this situation are primarily vertical, as there isn't any other direction to expand. The foreground may best be defined by a high horizontal framing element, such as the limb of a tree or a horizontal beam that is part of some other structure. An accelerated or intensified vanishing point in a false perspective, mimicking a segment of a steep and narrow gorge, could also be useful here. Place the stones in the composition so that the lines or planes implied along the tops of the stones (see page 54) all point toward the same focal point. Although this focal point can be a decorative element, it's most dramatic as a cave or dark depression, which suggests to viewers that the site continues beyond the visible space. You'll need to elevate the land on either side of the site significantly so that the sides descend toward and frame the line of sight to the focal point.

A deep and narrow site

This is equivalent to walking down a corridor or alley. The end of the site needs to be obscured — try using a bush, tree, or stone — and the visual or physical path should meander. Consider incorporating stones in sharp vertical descent or ascent along the edges to help direct the viewer's eye down the length of the space and break up the otherwise uninteresting flat planes of the sides.

CONTEXT AND MOTIVATION

Although in reality there is a significant order within the natural realm, to the uneducated eye it seems random and chaotic. Thus when we attempt to mimic the patterns of nature, we tend to either imbue them with our linear sense of order, or express them with little or no understanding of the system that underlies natural forms. When stones are spaced correctly, they reflect a natural *motivation* around a common occurrence or underlying theme. This motivation is part of what gives the entire grouping a relationship among its elements and to its environment.

These two relationships — that among the stones in the composition, and that between the composition and the environment in which it is placed — can be thought of as *context*. It is created by the motivation of the composition; in other words, proper motivation is the underlying theme that gives context or meaning to any stone composition, and it is crucial to that composition's success.

A common mistake made by designers struggling with the placement of stones is looking at the stones as individual elements rather than parts of a greater whole. If they are to look natural, stones must be spaced in the garden to appear unified in context and motivation. If they are not placed with a vision of the group as a whole, they are likely to seem random and unorganized. *Spacing* refers to the relative distances among stones in the ground or in water. Although proper spacing helps create dynamic tension among the objects (see page 55), its most important role is to create a sense of naturalness. People tend to place objects together in contrived formats. Repeating patterns and regular grids seem to show up frequently. You hear terms such as *four-square* pattern and *diamond* pattern expressed in discussions of Western landscape design. We tend to mimic the environment around us, which for most of us (as city dwellers) is composed of straight lines and square corners, and feel comfortable surrounding ourselves with a sense of order. The natural world is much more varied and complex than that. When you've decided what the motivation behind your stonescape will be, take time to study it and find out how it's truly shaped, the forces that have shaped it, what it has been, and the dynamics of its evolution.

The eroding desert mountain at top reveals the dynamics of erosion. The stone composition below it mimics this natural force and reflects excellent use of internal, external, and bioregional contexts that shape its motivation of a mountain.

As discussed on page 40, odd numbers work very well together when you're arranging stones; the most effective groupings have either three, five, seven, or nine stones. In a good stonescape, you will space these stones so that your composition could stand alone at any of these stages. In other words, it should be a complete picture with three stones as well as five stones, or seven stones, or nine. Understanding this will help you choose the order in which your stone grouping grows.

As it relates to the use of stones in the landscape, context can be thought of in three veins: internal, external, and bioregional.

Internal Context

Think of *internal context* as building a relationship among all the stones in your grouping. If you think of a stone arrangement as a single, solid mass of stone that has been eroded away over a long period of time, you will have a better idea of how to create your composition. Think about how the wind and water would affect that great stone mass, and place individual stones to reflect such effects. Each piece has a relationship to every other piece as well as to the whole. The most important ways that you can establish those relationships are through:

- Lines of force
- Repetition of line and form
- Implied planes
- Dynamic spacing
- Plantings

Lines of Force

Lines of force are invisible lines of energy that guide the formation of a natural stonescape. They are similar to the flux that surrounds a magnet — you don't see the lines of flux, but you do see their effect. If you sprinkle iron filings on some paper with a magnet underneath, those filings will align themselves in a pattern that outlines the invisible lines of flux exuded by the magnet. When you apply the same thinking to a stone arrangement, you establish a series of imaginary lines of force. These lines will be arranged into patterns, with one, two, or multiple lines in each. When you imagine these lines of force on the surface of the ground you are working on, the pictures that come to mind could include vertical, horizontal, diagonal, arcing, plumelike, and fan-shaped lines. These lines of force can occur on both an internal and external level.

External lines of force that influence the layout of your stones are derived from looking at the stones from a plan or overhead view. They create the logical sequence connecting the stones in a group. There are often two or three external lines of force connecting and making sense of the arrangement of the stones. In nature, these lines of force are readily apparent because they hint at the underlying form of the parent mass to which the surface stone is connected. In many of the plan drawings that appear later in this book (which show the layout from above), you will notice an overlay of connecting lines. These lines serve as guides for creating external lines of force in each composition.

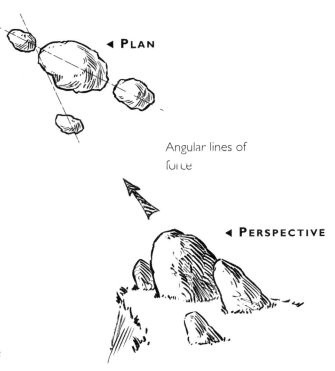

Angular lines of force

Internal lines of force are the motivating force behind the development of a stone formation. They can be likened to an explosive energy causing movement of mass to occur in the direction that the energy is focused. For example, if a composition's internal line of force is a strong vertical based below the ground, then its influence on the design of the group is the simulation of a pushing-upward motion. If the internal line of force is diagonal to the ground plane and its source is formed below that ground plane, the movement of the stones will tend to follow that angle. If the lines of force are based in the form of an expanding sphere, the stones will appear to radiate from a common point below the surface. By coordinating all such elements in a stone composition to face in a particular direction, you provide a unity or internal context that is based on the motivation of movement. The stone formation shown on page 51 maintains internal context not only through the implied planes that create the illusion that these stones were all once part of a larger mass, but also through the sense of movement or great force behind the upward thrust of the vertical stones.

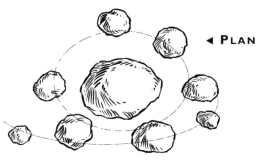

Radial lines of force

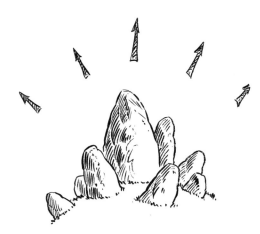

▲ **PERSPECTIVE**

Repeating lines, planes, and forms in fissures and formations are common in natural stone formations and will help create a sense of naturalness and unity in your composition.

Repetition of Lines and Forms

A good way to create a relationship among stones is to repeat certain lines and forms that are found in the dominant stone of the grouping. This relationship may be based on the angle of that stone in the ground, angles of fracture lines in its surface, or even its basic form. Repetition creates a clear relationship among all of the stones through that shared feature. Often the lines and forms will follow the lines of force that you have established, but sometimes you can also create a dramatic effect by using contrasting lines and forms.

Implied Planes

Implied means "suggested," and a *plane* is a flat surface. So in other words, an *implied plane* is an imaginary flat surface that is suggested to exist among the top lines of stones in a group. The general feeling an implied plane creates is that the stones are remnants of a larger single stone mass, and that time and erosion have worn away that mass to create the space between the stones in the arrangement.

This is a powerful way of sending a subconscious message to the viewer that all the stones in the group are related by way of origin. More important, it also tells the viewer that this is defined place, not just a random grouping of stones. In this light, you can better see how to use a mountain as the motivation for your stonescape: Create implied planes among the stones that allude to a larger precursor.

Implied planes help to connect different stones in a grouping, and can suggest that they are remnants of a former larger geological formation.

Dynamic Spacing

Dynamic spacing is placement that anticipates some form of dynamic action, such as a piece of an iceberg caught in the act of breaking away.

A stone composition with good dynamic spacing seems to indicate a suspended moment in a process of great movement or energy. Creating a relationship, or *dynamic tension,* among stones through the use of dynamic spacing is thus more of a challenge than the use of implied planes, lines of force, or repetition of lines and forms. If you place the stones too far apart, viewers will not recognize the potential dynamic. If you place the stones too close together, it will seem to the viewers that the "action" has already happened. If you space the stones properly, however, the sense of imminent action will help cement the whole piece together as a single composition.

Too far apart

Too close together

Good dynamic tension

Plantings

Plantings are another way to create an internal context. Massing of plants can provide a connective texture that ties your stones together as a unit, reinforcing any unity that you have established with your choice of geological or natural motivation. Part of the beauty of stones in a planted environment is that they become foils against which to play the texture, colors, and forms of the plants. This does not just apply to a land environment. In a water's-edge environment, your plantings might be cotton grass, sedges, or cattails; in an underwater environment, water lilies or lotuses. In some situations, your plant material may actually suggest what size stones to choose relative to the space you are working in to successfully create an internal context.

Plantings can not only lend internal context to a stone grouping, but also help define the underlying motivation of the stones.

Placing smaller stones that mimic the angle of an existing larger stone can create a connection to the surrounding environment (external context) through a sense of movement.

Multiple implied planes build a sense of movement toward the focal-point statue. To further enhance external context, the statue should reflect the architectural style of its environment.

External Context

External context refers to the relationship between the stonescape and the external environment within which it resides. A stone grouping will seem out of context if it does not feel connected to the land or surroundings in some way. You can create external context in a variety of ways, but the primary methods are movement, architectural elements, and plantings.

Movement

If your composition implies movement through internal lines of force, you can select the direction of movement from the surrounding landscape. For example, if a nearby tree has a particular lean, you can mimic that angle in your stone composition. Another way is to use the movement you've created to lead the viewer's eye toward some point of interest — a view, a framed opening, or even a statue.

Architectural Elements

Architectural elements are another way of establishing an external context. If the architecture of your home (or your client's) is of a distinctive style or historical era, use objects that reflect that style or era within the body of your composition. If the house is early American, for instance, consider the use of a hand pump and bucket with a recirculating pump. If the house is of the Spanish-style adobe common in the southwestern United States, you could consider including a wagon wheel or cow skull.

Plantings

Plantings can be another way of creating an external continuity and context. By blending the plant palette in the existing landscape with that of your stone composition, you imply that all of this belongs together, creating a sense of connection. Also, if any small trees or shrubs are outside the site of the stone grouping but still visible, you should repeat at least one of those trees or shrubs in your composition.

Bioregional Context

An important type of context that is often ignored is bioregional context. The region you live in has its own character and its own expression of the geological form. If at all possible, this should serve as the motivation for the dynamics of the stone grouping you create. It will give your design a better sense of place, and will ground it in the local environment. You might think of it as native-space definition and celebration. Native plants, used in conjunction with stones that reflect the geology of the region, can reinforce your composition's bioregional context.

WORKING WITH RATIOS

One of the first things you should know about ratios is that most people have a certain "gut" response, positive or negative, to the way objects are laid out. This spatial relationship can be referred to as the *dynamics of the space*. The emotional reactions can range from a warm and fuzzy feeling to breaking down and crying from the beauty of it. Such widely differing responses to the same place are due in large part to the different experiences, levels of awareness, states of mind, and relative sensitivity of the viewers. But in every case, the space with arranged objects "spoke to them" and affected them at some emotional level. Proper use of ratios in a composition is what makes that space dynamic and allows it to "speak" to that emotional awareness of viewers.

A *ratio* can best be described as a mathematical relationship between two measurements. It can refer to the relationship between the height of one object and the length of another, or the relationship between the length of one object and the width of another. For a single object, the term *ratio* generally refers to the relationship between its height and its width. With stonescapes, of course, *height, width*, and *length* refer to the dimensions of the stones as they will be ultimately placed. Ratios can also refer to the relationship between the size of the object and the size of the environment in which it will be placed.

When you use ratios as a consideration in design, you need to look at those ratios relative to your viewing position. As this viewing position changes, so does the appearance of those objects to each other. A ratio critical to vertically oriented compositions is that of the height of the central element to the heights of the subordinate objects surrounding and seeking to establish a relationship with it. If there is no significant difference between the subordinate objects and the vertical focal point of the composition, it is unlikely that this element can act as a focal point. In addition, as the viewing position changes, the viewer won't see any dynamic interplay between the stones in the composition, thereby losing any emotional involvement with the space. However, if the subordinate objects are too low relative to the focal point, they can become lost, and the same principle applies.

Each element in the composition should contribute something to the whole, regardless of the format. To look at the entire composition as a whole is dealing with the issue more on the level of rhythm (see page 60). Dealing with it on a stone-by-stone basis is a different story, and each ratio should be dealt with on an individual basis. Once the composition is settled in the ground, you can adjust the stones for the "total" picture.

Expressing Ratios

Ratios can be expressed as percentages or in a mathematical format. For example, the ratios between a single dominant object and several other subservient objects can be expressed as a series of ratios in a percentage form. The single dominant object is referred to as 100 percent. Each subsequent object is compared to the dominant, and the result expressed as a percentage of that standard. If the dominant stone is 3 units in height and the second stone is 2 units high, the second stone is 66 percent of the dominant feature. A third stone that is 1 unit in height is 33 percent, and so on.

When you compare the height and width of a single object, the mathematical format takes precedence. For example, if a stone is 4 units high and 1 unit wide, the ratio is 4:1. If it's 6 units high and 2 units wide, the ratio is 6:2 or, simplified even further, 3:1.

Vertical-to-Vertical Ratios

Example 1

Stone	Percentage
1	100%
2	62%
3	38%
4	24%
5	15%

Example 2

Stone	Percentage
1	100%
2	50%
3	20%
4	75%
5	35%

Example 3

Stone	Percentage
1	100%
2	75%
3	40%
4	30%
5	30%

Example 4

Stone	Percentage
1	100%
2	40%
3	90%
4	60%
5	20%

Example 5

Stone	Percentage
1	100%
2	75%
3	45%
4	20%
5	20%

The boxes on this and the facing page give a number of ratios for five-stone arrangements that work nicely, and two examples from each are illustrated. The vertical-to-vertical ratios compare the heights of stones in a grouping, and the horizontal-to-horizontal ratios compare the lengths. The numbers refer to the stone-setting sequence, and all of the ratios listed are in reference to the first stone. For instance, in example 1 of the vertical-to-vertical ratios, if stone 1 is 38 inches (or centimeters) tall, then it follows that stone 2 is 24 inches (cm) tall; stone 3 is 15 inches (cm) tall; stone 4 is 9 inches (cm) tall; and stone 5 is 6 inches (cm) tall. As you begin planning your layout, use these sample ratios to help you choose your stones. Experimentation will lead you to other ratios that are equally pleasing.

Vertical-to-Vertical Example 1

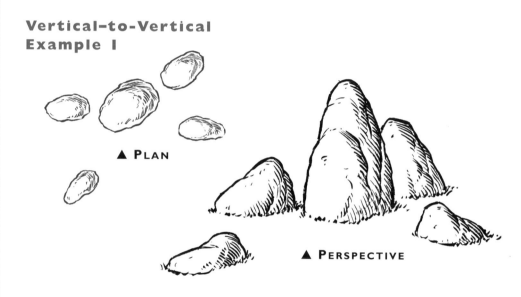

▲ PLAN

▲ PERSPECTIVE

Vertical-to-Vertical Example 3

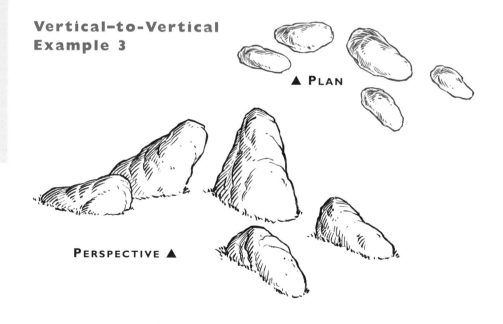

▲ PLAN

PERSPECTIVE ▲

Horizontal-to-Horizontal Ratios

| Example 1 | | Example 2 | | Example 3 | | Example 4 | | Example 5 | |
Stone	Percentage	Stone	Percentage	Stone	Percentage	Stone	Percentage	Stone	Percentage
1	100%	1	100%	1	100%	1	100%	1	100%
2	70%	2	70%	2	55%	2	75%	2	70%
3	50%	3	50%	3	20%	3	60%	3	50%
4	55%	4	50%	4	40%	4	40%	4	40%
5	45%	5	30%	5	35%	5	30%	5	20%

The natural motivation for creating a grouping of stones that vary in height is weathering and erosion patterns. The true effectiveness of the ratios is played out only in the relationships among the stones, including the general form of each stone and how that stone becomes related to a companion stone.

In these examples, the numbers have been rounded to the nearest inch. Some people are sticklers for precision, but we have discovered that the other factors, such as spacing and context, can be more important. In other words, the ultimate criteria are the eye of the beholder and sensitivity to what works. Bear this in mind as you play out the sample ratios given here.

Horizontal-to-Horizontal Example 2

◀ PLAN

◀ PERSPECTIVE

Horizontal-to-Horizontal Example 4

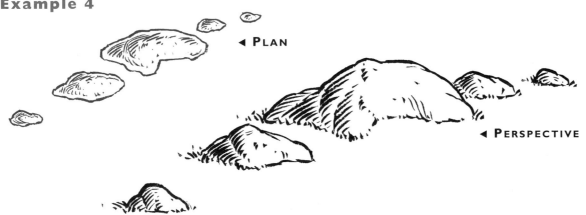

◀ PLAN

◀ PERSPECTIVE

CREATING RHYTHM, STYLE, AND EMPHASIS

The appearance of well-placed stones can be aptly described as the visual equivalent of a musical composition. In a piece of music, the rhythm is played out note by note along a time line, whereas the rhythm of stones in a grouping is a whole symphony that is visible as an entire piece. As with music, the relationship of the elements (musical notes/stones) to each other affects how we feel, and the manner or style in which the composition is played has the most influence on how people respond to it. The rhythm of a polka, jug band music, or a marching band will create in most people a desire to dance or at least tap their feet. It can be said that the music resonates within them and they feel a certain sense of joy. Music that is more sedate evokes a somber and reflective feeling, again due to the timing and style of the playing of the notes.

The same principles of rhythm that rule in music can be applied to the relationship of objects to each other. Using stones of all the same size spaced evenly apart and sitting atop the ground is equivalent to playing a long and drawn-out single note on an instrument — no interest, no purpose, no feelings outside of monotony. This is not a meaningful composition, yet it is a very common arrangement of stones in the landscape. By using the metaphor of musical rhythm and style, however, you can arrange stones according to different design concepts:

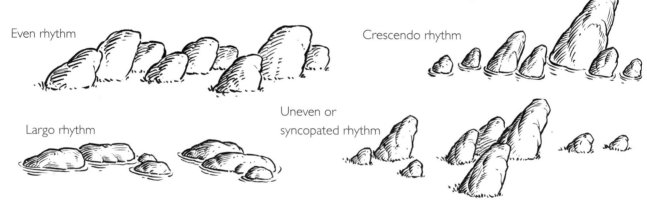

Even rhythm

Crescendo rhythm

Largo rhythm

Uneven or syncopated rhythm

- **Even.** A collection of stones that repeat a regular pattern; as the pattern repeats, it grows, and it does so with a style or character appropriate to the overall site.
- **Uneven** or **Syncopated.** An erratic (but still directional) piece that is tied together by subtle lines and patterns, and an overall sense of growth; usually employs implied planes.
- **Crescendo.** A sharply ascending vertical composition in which all stones point in the direction of the pinnacle stone.
- **Largo.** A composition of large, flat stones that rise within softly arced mounds.

One of the best examples of rhythm in natural stone groupings is the way stones appear on the shore of a lake or ocean. Natural forces of wind and water movement, seasonal forces such as ice, and the historical influence of glaciers can all contribute to the story behind these dynamic natural compositions.

In the case of a rocky lake shore or beach-front, the stones establish not only a vertical rhythm along the horizontal shoreline but also a sense of depth relative to that shoreline. When viewed from the water at shoreline, some stones are firmly embedded in the upper background while others have fallen forward into the lower foreground. If the shore is viewed from above, a separate rhythm appears, one quite distinct from the vertical rhythm of the stones when viewed from the water. This time, some stones are firmly embedded back from the shoreline, and others have fallen or moved out into the water. In places where a large stone might separate from the shore (such as a cliff), there are likely to be relatively large stones extending out into the body of the lake. Seen from above like this, you could trace the natural external lines of force linking all the stones on the shore.

Typically, when people try to duplicate the appearance of rocks around a body of water, they incorrectly use stones of all the same size and texture and place them only along the very edge of the shore. If you instead place larger stones back from the edge, put some stones into the water near the edge, and even submerge some elements, you will come closer to capturing the natural appearance of a rocky shoreline. In addition, if you vary the sizes of your stones, you will enhance the overall appearance and more closely reflect the characteristics of a water-and-stone edge in nature.

To build a waterside stonescape, think about these rhythms along the lake shore and ocean beach. Try to understand why the stones are where they are to begin with. There is a motivation or reason behind each natural composition, and by understanding the process that brought it into being, you can find a basis for how you as a designer will create your composition.

This small stone peninsula reaching into the water echoes the larger peninsula in the distance. Notice how the peninsula dips down and slips into the water while the rhythmic energy of its rocky exterior creates a sense of life and movement carried through the expanse of time.

A monotonous ring of stones around a pond has no rhythm and is obviously artificial.

An appropriate rhythm of large to small stones that fall into and out from the pond's edge is more natural in appearance.

MAINTAINING BALANCE

As a design consideration in the placement of stones, balance can be thought of in two lights: structural layout and groundedness. *Balance in structural layout* refers to a formal or an informal parallelism or symmetry. *Grounded balance* refers to just how stable something feels or appears. Does the group seem out of balance? Is it well grounded? Will it fall over? Does it seem top-heavy? These are all questions you would ask when considering how stable something is. The best way to avoid an ungrounded and out-of-balance situation is to adhere to the rules of formal and informal balance.

Formal Balance

A formal balance is one that is linear and symmetrical in structure. If you place a number of elements together in a formally balanced arrangement, you would likely be able to draw a line through the center of the composition and be left with two mirror-image sides. This creates a great sense of stability, which is enhanced as you add a sense of depth to the objects. Most early Western landscape design used this approach. Notable exceptions include the naturalistic designers Andrew Jackson Downing, Jens Jenson, O. C. Simonds, and Frederick Law Olmsted, who used an informal approach based more on the rhythms of nature.

Formally balanced compositions are usually symmetrical in nature and create the impression of utmost stability.

Informal Balance

Informal balance is not nearly as easy to achieve when planning the layout of a stone group. One approach to establishing informal balance is to draw an imaginary line through a portion of where the stone composition will be set. If there is on one side of that line a tall vertical stone, then there should be a low flat stone on the other side of the line to balance it out. If there is a large chunky type of stone on one side of the line, there should be some smaller chunky types on the opposite side that are equal in total mass to the large stone.

In this composition, the large chunky stone on the right is informally balanced against several smaller chunky stones on the right.

REVIEWING SCALE

The scale of a stone composition to its site and viewers is also important to the design. Good use of scale makes a grouping feel as though it "belongs" in its surroundings, enhancing its visual appeal and attraction. Good use of scale is a subtle touch, however — its absence is far more noticeable than its presence.

Relative to the Site

The proper use of scale helps make a stone grouping seem appropriate to the size of its site. One common mistake is not considering the surroundings or dimensions of the visual space within which the stone grouping is placed. For instance, imagine you have a stone grouping on a flat surface overlooked by a kitchen area, a patio, or even a corporate cafeteria. If there is nothing behind that grouping containing the space, the eye will stop briefly on the arrangement, then zoom on out and beyond. In order to dominate such a landscape, the grouping's scale would have to be massive in order to stop the eye. Similarly, imagine the same kitchen (or patio or cafeteria) but instead of empty space beyond, there is a massive stone cliff. Now the problem is one of conflicting scale. The background appears to dominate the scene. The stones in the composition should relate to the texture and color of the cliff, and there should be a logical transition from the cliff to the grouping. In regard to scale, however, the sizes of the stones need to be in conjunction with the sizes of the fissure and fault lines evident in the cliff face.

The stones in this arrangement are too small for the scale of space intimated by the huge pillars of concrete. In this situation, a designer should use massive vertical stones to match the lines and scale of the columns, or long horizontal stones to mirror the lines of the wall in the background and balance the tremendous vertical relief of the pillars.

If a space is narrow and long, such as a shallow back- or side yard, the maximum height you can deal with has to be scaled to the height of the typical observer. In this environment, you also have to be careful to include a sufficient range of transition in the narrow depth you are working in. One way to do this is to intrude on the visible foreground space by placing a slightly larger stone just beyond a confining barrier (such as a fence or wall) and then repeating the form of that stone in the midground — but at 62 percent of the background stone's height relative to the ground plane.

Transition and depth are key in creating a sense of scale for a long, narrow site.

Relative to People

Scale relative to people is generally a factor when viewers are intimate with a landscape that is meant to convey a sense of a larger space. This can happen in two different ways: physical entry and close proximity.

When you physically enter the space where the stone composition resides, two things happen. First, if you are standing next to the stone grouping, any illusion that a designer may have been attempting to achieve in regard to false scale is ruined for you. Second, anyone who sees you or anyone else adjacent to the stone composition is also subject to having that illusion destroyed: Either anyone standing near the formation will look to be the size of Godzilla, or the stone grouping will diminish in its strength and power. The latter is usually the case. For this reason, it is a good idea to restrict access into spaces where this could happen.

In the case of close proximity, people cannot physically enter the designed environment, but they can come very close to its space — which is relatively narrow, with no opportunity to create significant depth. In such a situation, we recommend that you use massive stone features to effectively communicate the emotions of the composition. Imagine an outdoor sitting and eating area, for instance, that is next to the area where you will be creating your stone grouping. You want something that will tower above the diners and create a more intimate scale for the spaces they will occupy. An option, if you don't have access to massive stones and cranes, is to lower the "ceiling" of the space by incorporating trees into the plaza and, especially, around the edge of the viewed space. This creates a relatively low horizontal framing line that will allow you to employ some space-compression tricks.

CREATING ILLUSIONS

Many times, the use of stone compositions in a landscape is about creating an illusion within the space that you are designing for. Usually, it is one of two illusions: making a small space look large, or making a large space look small.

Making a Small Space Look Large

Making a small space appear large means dealing with scale on an intimate level. The simplest method is to subtly reduce the size of objects. For instance, if a stepping-stone pathway runs alongside your work area, you want to be sure of three things: one, that there is limited access; two, that the largest stepping-stones are about two-thirds the size of normal ones; and three, that all subsequent stepping-stones slowly reduce in size (down to about half normal size) as they move farther into the distance. Work your stones' sizes and formations in relation to this scale.

A small backyard can be made to appear larger with a stone composition that mimics much larger stone formations often found in nature, and a space that continues beyond the viewer's line of sight.

Another technique is to create spaces that go somewhere visually — but the viewer cannot see exactly where. This creates the feeling that there is more space beyond. Try a path that disappears around a bend, or a rising hillock with open space beyond it.

Such spaces work best as viewed places, not spaces viewers can physically enter. If you wish to succeed in the illusion, it is critical to get your ratios correct — if you are modeling after a natural scene and they are wrong, all illusion is suspended and the formation looks out of place. Sometimes simply moving stones closer together by a matter of inches is all it takes to make things right. You also need to use plants of a fine texture in combination with the stone. Large-textured plants (those with large and/or dense leaves) make the place more intimate and will only help destroy the scale.

Making a Large Space Look Small

This is as much of a challenge to pull off as is its opposite. It involves the use of large-textured plants and focused viewsheds. The latter are well-framed large-scale landscape compositions. These environments are actually fun to enter, and can have an interesting emotional impact on you. You begin to feel younger, since your body remembers environments like this from when you were a child and half the size you are now. Before

attempting this approach, it is important that you really understand the dynamics and dimensions of "normal" space. The use of false perspective in viewsheds is very important to overall success. Stone groupings need to be larger, yet must maintain a proper sense of proportion to the landscape and employ proper ratios among themselves. When proportionate to the landscape, the large stones of the groupings will help to scale down a viewer's perception of the space, and enhance the illusion.

To see how the distortion in this large space works, place your thumb over the house — the landscape and stone groupings look small, as if they might appear in a suburban backyard. Remove your thumb, and you can see how enormous the space really is. To maintain this illusion, place an obfuscating element, such as a tree or bush, so that it blocks the view of the house from the primary perspective. As viewers approach the house, they see an average landscape. When they step away from the primary perspective (perhaps following the path around a bend), they see the house and realize the scope of the illusion.

Distortions

Although an intimate landscape may at first seem confining, it allows you to have some fun with stones by creating spatial distortions. By accelerating the false perspectives from one or both ends of the designed space, you can create some interesting environments. If you use a spacing that is even and regular but increases in size as the stones become larger, you can emphasize the feeling of depth within the composition. If you do this in a vertical as well as a horizontal format, the distortion of space is very effective. Take pictures of subjects at opposite ends to get a true feel for what is happening.

One way of compressing and distorting space is very effective in a narrow and long space. This might be along a fence, a house, or a line of trees in a lawn adjacent to the street. If the primary point of view is from the side, your goal is to create a relatively steep ascension of line. Closest to the viewed edge should be a very low ground plane; adjacent to the viewed edge (moving into the space), the ground plane should rise rapidly. The basic tricks lies in creating foreground, midground, and background elements, all within a very confined space. Stones can be used for all of these, but usually a fence that is slightly forward of the back of the space is the most effective to create background, leaving the stones for foreground and midground. Place a design element (such as a tree) behind that fence to give the illusion that there is more space behind it.

As described above, simple distortion such as this is a great tool for opening up a limited space.

DESIGNING AROUND SITE AMENITIES

At times, your design will be dictated by your site. If there are preexisting site amenities, they may lend themselves to becoming an environment where stones as objects or grouping could work very effectively. Three common hardscape features that can lead to some interesting design solutions are walks, patios, and walls (both retaining and freestanding).

Walks

Walks can be broken into two basic styles: formal and informal.

Formal walks are generally very linear and are constructed of a consistent medium, such as wood, brick, ashlar stone, poured or stamped concrete, or concrete pavers. Incorporating accent stone into a formal walk is a good way to emphasize the formality of that walk. By breaking into the line of the walk and placing boulders and stones into its area of control (the surface of the walk), you create the illusion that the walkway was originally built around this stone formation. It gives significant credibility to the motivation of the stones, and it emphasizes the pervasiveness of the formal design element (the formal walk). The one thing you have to consider is the cost of modifying that existing walk to embrace the stones. This will likely involve cutting brick or concrete and then reworking it to look as though it had never been disturbed. The result, however, can be well worth the cost.

▼ **PERSPECTIVE**

In an informal walk or path, stones can serve a couple of functions. Stones adjacent to the path can act as a motivation for the various turns of the path. A winding path is sometimes placed in a woodland environment, but at other times it seems to wind for absolutely no reason other than people think it should. While it is true that a meandering path is more appealing than an arrow-straight one, if there is no reason for the twists and turns, it is out of context with its environment. If you place a stone or a group of stones within the space where you are planning your path, however, that pathway will naturally interact with those stones. Your approach should be determined by the primary point of view of those stones — although you also need to

▼ **PLAN**

The intrusion of accent stones or a small composition into a formal path lends credence and stature to the formality of that path, creating an atmosphere of a strictly formal landscape imposed upon an informally opposed land.

consider the perspective when you are coming down the path from the opposite direction. If you have an existing winding path, place the stone compositions or solitary elements as would be appropriate for the dynamics of that particular walk.

In both formal and informal types of walkways, you have the opportunity to visually tie several solitary stones and stone groupings together. Arrange the stones in one group so that they naturally lead the eye to the next group, and so on. This can give an interesting common thread to the entire path. Another way to approach a larger composition that is only seen one piece at a time is to create the illusion of some larger underlying geological formation. Establish apparent veins of stone that run in the same direction. The path works its way through the space, discovering a series of similar formations. This can also help provide a sense of place.

▼ **PLAN**

▼ **PERSPECTIVE**

The stones in this composition provide an informal motivation for the twists and turns of the walkway. The meandering path seems to wind its way through the remnants of a larger geological formation.

Patios

A patio can be thought of as a flat horizontal plane upon which social activities take place. There are several environments within a patio that are well suited to the inclusion of stone groupings or even solitary stone elements. The first type of contrived environment has either a solitary stone acting as a focal point, or several tall standing stones used to create a dynamic tension within the space, giving the patio a sense of place. Leave open space around the stones for plantings, and open up some of the paving element to include similar plantings there as well. If you use a single stone, ideally it should be fairly vertical and about the size of an adult. A grouping of stones should include a family of diminishing sizes, to give a feeling of physical transformation that implies great age.

▼ **PLAN**

▼ **PERSPECTIVE**

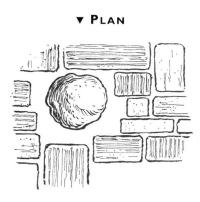

Vertical stones embedded in a patio can serve as focal points; to enhance the focus, open up the pavement around them for plantings.

The second environment in a patio that lends itself to the inclusion of stones is its edge. Stones placed here should be relatively flat, to complement the plane of the patio. Several stones that ascend from the ground level are best. Separation between the stones is helpful; here, you can plant perennials and dwarf shrubs into what appear to be fissures and cracks of a larger stone formation. Place the stone that is closest to the edge of the patio to reach about 2 feet (60 cm) or so above the patio. This can serve as a bench or sitting area. The stone that rises behind this should either be massive or about shoulder height when sitting. If you use a shoulder height stone, planting shrub masses behind it will create a greater sense of depth.

PERSPECTIVE ▼

▼ PLAN

The stones in this composition ascend gradually from the ground plane of the patio. In addition, the lower stones are just the right height to serve as seats.

The third stone environment for a patio is embedded stone, which creates the illusion that the patio was built around it. Like pathways, this lends itself to the idea that these stones are part of an underlying geological formation. Whatever your paving material is, try to keep it as close to the stones as possible. If you choose your stones wisely, they can also double as patio furniture.

▼ PERSPECTIVE

▼ PLAN

Stone groupings embedded in the middle of a patio can create the impression that they belong to a tremendous underground geologic formation that was too big to be moved, so the patio was built around it.

A retaining wall modeled after nature will create the impression that the stones are shifting with the movements of the earth and the vagaries of the weather.

Walls

There are two types of wall, and both lend themselves to the use of stones as objects: retaining walls and freestanding walls.

A *retaining wall* keeps soil and earth from intruding on another surface, usually a flat plane. When you're designing a stone composition that will serve as a retaining wall, you might use as your model the edge of a northern lake shore resplendent in stone. Such a shore is essentially a snapshot of Mother Nature at work; in it, you can see the impact of the various forces that influence our physical geography. Primary among these forces is water — not liquid, but rather in the form of ice. When the glaciers (ice) made their retreat, they left behind stones embedded in the soil. The frozen lake (ice) has a tendency to move and shift, causing these stones to break away from the shore and dislodge others to the point where they are almost totally in the water — in some cases totally submerged. The stones are not uniform in size or color, but do show a consistency of form. They tend to be rounded to elongated, with little angularity. An understanding of this rhythm of size and placement relative to the shoreline is critical to creating a wall with a similar feeling. Some stones should be set farther back from the wall, on the earth being retained, and others pushed forward from the wall, on the ground plane. Use creeping plants along the edge of the new retaining wall to further establish the wall's sense of permanence and longevity.

A *freestanding stone wall* is primarily a design conceit, simply establishing the mid-ground, framing, or even hiding a view. The challenge comes in working with a large number of stones; you may find it difficult to make them seem unified. However, it is critical that there be a unifying motivation for the general form of this wall, or it will look like just a bunch of rocks. It needs to be expressive and distinct. One good way is to interweave an interesting textural mass of plants to try to create a feeling of movement.

By massing the long, low horizontal stones in the midground and mirroring the vertical stones of the foreground with stones in the background, this freestanding wall appears unified. A low, shrubby plant could also be planted in and limited to the area occupied by the wall to further the effect.

CREATIVE APPLICATIONS

Using stones as objects in the landscape, whether a single stone or an inspired composition, is creative in its own right. However, you can go still further without compromising the quality and integrity of what you do. Listed below are a few more stonescaping suggestions.

Stacking Stones

Stacking stones has been popular with numerous cultures across the globe; such stacks have been used as cairns, burials, trail markers, and pure decoration. If you think of stacking stones as artistic, you can see where you might have a lot of fun with it. One very important word of caution: Stacked stones that are not cemented together in some fashion can and do fall. They can be defined as attractive nuisances that particularly endanger children, who see them as really neat playground equipment. In other words, be very careful about the environment in which you use stacked stones; make sure they are secure from tampering and will not cause any injury.

Round stones are the most difficult to work with and therefore more of a challenge. If you like challenges, you will love trying to create meaningful compositions with rounded stones. One way to approach this is not to think about stacking straight up; rather, create slowly arcing curvilinear masses. Use larger and darker stones toward the bottom, and smaller, lighter ones near the top. The lines of force you create can lead the eye very effectively.

Curvilinear masses of stacked round stones create arcing lines of force that lead the eye up and away from the ground plane.

Flat stones are much easier to stack, and there are a considerable number of directions you can go using stacked flat stones as a focal point. Consider making a freestanding wall with strategically placed openings of various sizes along its face. Putting votive candles into the selective openings can create a broad range of responses when the work is viewed at night. Another possibility is to stack flat stones in an overlapping fashion to create bowls with circular openings. Make some concave, others convex. Put plants or objets d'art within them to add more interest; you could even place electric lights in the recesses you make. The only limit is your imagination.

Stacked flat stones allow openings in which you can place candles, small electric lights, or decorative items.

From the outside, the stones in this rod-tied stack seem precariously perched, ready to topple at the first breeze.

In the first approach to using mass stone as a focal point, set all the stones so that they lead the eye toward the primary stone, as if it were a stone magnet.

In the second approach, angle the stones away from the primary stone, increasing the pitch as you descend. The dynamic of lines and planes enhances the stature of the primary stone — it seems as if it were repelling the other stones.

Another interesting way to stack stones (either all one type of stone, or a mixture of forms) is in a gravity-defying column, using a steel rod to hold each stone in place on top of each other so that the stacks seem to twist in impossible directions. Twist a sturdy steel rod to an interesting form, and place it securely into the ground or in poured cement so that it is very stable. Then in the stones, drill holes slightly larger in diameter than the rod. Slip the stones over the rod one at a time. The result can be fascinating. The most effective of these stacks creates a dynamic tension in which viewers think it may just be possible for those stones to be stacked together but the slightest gust of wind could topple them. Try either a very slightly arching stack, or a reverse pyramid in which the smallest stones are on the bottom, and stones become progressively larger the higher they are.

Vertical Masses

If you want to create a vertical focal point that is unique, try massing a great deal of stones together with some unifying theme.

Start by building a steep mound in the place you have chosen for your focal point. You need to have collected a large quantity of stones that are all of the same basic character, texture, and shape. The sizes can vary and, for the best arrangement, they should represent a broad range of dimensions. Place the largest and most attractive stone at the top of the mound, then start adding all of the other stones in the same vertical format as the first one.

There are two approaches to take from this point. You can either have each of your subsequent stones point toward the first one, or you can point each subsequent stone away from the first with the angle of pitch increasing as you move down the mound. The final stones in this second approach may be more than 60 degrees off the vertical. Also, as you descend from the center of the mound, the distance between the stones should increase. Whereas the first stone may be almost touching the ones next to it, the last stones may be several feet from each other. A good technique is to double the distance each time you place a succeeding lower section. Finally, plant the entire space with a ground cover that is fairly uniform in texture.

Yamadoro

Japanese *Yamadoro* lanterns are unique and creative ornaments for the landscape. *Yama* means "mountain" and *doro* means "lantern," so essentially the phrase can be translated as "mountain lantern." These stone-

sheltered candles should be set where they can be seen — especially at night — but where they aren't liable to be tipped over.

Such lanterns are a lot of fun to construct. You need to keep your eye out for certain types of stone, however, in order to make an effective one. Start with the base, which should be fairly broad, thick, and flat. Next comes the pedestal — a rectangular upright piece that is flat on both ends is good, but a squarish block would work as effectively. You then need the bottom of the actual lantern; it should ideally be broad and flat, and it should balance easily on top of the pedestal piece. Two or three smaller stones come next, serving to shelter the candle and support the top of the lantern. The top of the lantern should be of a similar configuration as the pedestal, except at least half again as broad. Finally, place two smaller stones atop the broad cap. These serve to finish off the piece and actually do enhance its overall appearance.

From a safety perspective, you may want to consider drilling holes through all of the pieces and putting a stabilizing rod through the whole lantern.

This well-designed garden illustrates many of the design principles we've discussed. The grounds are easily discernible: the path spills into a shallow foreground, which is separated from the background by the unmown barrier of the midground, helping to create a sense of great depth. Notice how the short vertical stone in the foreground adjacent to the path is mirrored in the mid- and background by two more vertical stones. The line drawn through these stones runs straight down the path toward the viewer, creating the fulcrum of balance that holds the arbor on the right and the shrubby tree on the left. Three flat-topped stones both frame the view of the arbor and chair as well as create an implied plane that leads directly to the unmown midground. The space of the garden is well-defined and framed by the mowed edges, hedges, and trees, and the masses of plantings running from and framing each area helps to imbue a sense of context and motivation, as does the repetition of stones of the same geological origin.

Choosing and Finding Your Stones

5

When you first go looking for stones to use in the landscape, you are apt to be surprised by either the lack of options or the vast quantity and diversity of stones on hand. Around the world, some areas are replete with stones of a wide variety of texture, structure, and form, while others have only one type. In those areas entirely devoid of rocky matter, there's no chance of confusion: You simply ship in the type of stone you want.

In order to make educated stone choices, you need to know what your potential palette of stone types is, including the basic forms in which they can be found. By organizing the stones in this manner, you can determine what will be best for your composition. In addition, you need to be aware of the subtler considerations of your site and the overall structure of your composition.

As a designer, you don't need a geologist's knowledge of all the different species of stone, their degrees of hardness, or the theories behind their formation. It is far more important to understand stones on the basis of their overall form or structure.

The outward appearance of a stone, whether it's alone or in a group, is largely determined by its geological roots and the types of erosion that influence it. The more you study stones and their forms, the greater your appreciation will become for the diversity of textures and shapes that exist in this "rocky realm." One of the first things you'll begin to notice is a repetition of surface patterns and outward forms, such as smooth, light, and mottled, or deeply grooved and linear. This repetition connects the stones in ways that can lend themselves to some truly inspired creations.

BASIC TYPES OF STONE

In order to bring a sense of order to the search for the right stones, it is helpful to break stones into specific families according to form. The vast majority of stones that you encounter in your search will fall into one or more of the following groups: rounded edges, pitted surface, angular edges, embedded elements, "married" stone, and artificial stones. Often you will find stones that are not dominated by any one of these elements, but rather fall into several categories simultaneously. For instance, you may discover a stone that has rounded edges with a pitted surface, and also contains embedded elements. You can focus on one of these elements as a common thread in creating your grouping or arrangement of stones. For instance, an embedded vein of white quartz could show up in many of your stones. If you choose this as your common thread or unifying factor, the other aspects of those stones will take on less importance as you determine how to group them.

Rounded Edges

Round- and smooth-edged stones are often shaped by moving water, and you can usually find them where swift rivers, glacial till, or the ocean tides are or have been. They can be very challenging to work with because their surfaces have no line of sight for creating implied planes, which can make it difficult to create a feeling of unity within the composition. In addition, these stones often vary significantly in color and tex-

The Origin of Stone

Geologists debate over how the earth was formed, but seem to agree on a time line involving billions of years. They believe that our planet began as a swirling mass of gas dust and debris. As atomic and gravitational forces worked on this mass, it began to cool, and formed a primordial crust atop an inner portion containing superheated liquids and gases. The gravitational pull trapped the gases in what was to become our atmosphere. As time passed, the crust became thicker and cooler, and floated on molten seas. The plates of cooled material moved into each other, creating violent impacts that pushed these sheets of material upward to form mountain ranges. Furthermore, geologists believe that icy comets crashed on the earth, creating steam. The primitive atmosphere trapped the steam, creating rain; oceans began to form. Meanwhile, the sheets of cooled material continued to collide in an ever-organizing chaos. Volcanoes formed, spewing their molten lava and cooling. Eventually the continents were formed.

It is during cooling stages that all rock was and is formed. Molten material called magma is the predecessor of stone. Rocks formed directly after this magma state are called *igneous*. When some of these rocks are in the right place at the right time to be compacted under tremendous pressure, they transform into *metamorphic* rocks. As natural forces of wind, rain, and gravity act upon these rocks, they break down into silts; silt deposits harden to form *sedimentary* rocks. Like igneous rocks, sedimentary rocks under high pressure are transformed into new metamorphic rocks. The three types of rock — igneous, metamorphic, and sedimentary — constitute all the stone on earth.

ture, which just adds to the challenge of creating internal context for a meaningful and pleasing arrangement.

When you first start to work with these stones, you will scratch your head trying to figure out ways to combine them that work. It can be done. Luckily, these stones are among the easiest to find in a very broad range of sizes, so you can use them in wonderful transitional groupings. By playing with the rhythm of the stones in arrangements, you will begin to find an endless array of expressions. This rhythm is usually best expressed by concentrating on ground spacing and establishing pleasing ratios among the relative heights of stones within the group.

Pitted Surface

Stones with a pitted surface are quite dramatic and can become good solitary focal points in the landscape. The pitted surfaces are a result of weathering. Sometimes this is due to weaker material being chemically etched away; in some formations, it's due to stones wearing on one another. One of the most famous types of pitted stone is the T'ai-hua stone of Chinese gardens. Looking like clouds, these mammoth, eroded limestone monoliths seem to float through the Chinese landscape, to good effect. Using them in arrangements works as well, although it may be difficult to find enough stones with similar characteristics to create an overriding internal context in your arrangement.

Pitted stones can range in appearance from the whimsical, ethereal quality of T'ai-hua stones (at right) to a porous, grainy surface (top) that looks almost acid-eaten.

This large angular stone contains many natural lines and planes that could easily be used to design lines of force or implied planes within a composition.

Angular Edges

Some stones have sharp, angular edges separating broad or narrow surface planes. The angles of these edges will vary according to the manner in which the stone was formed, the type of stone it is, and the way in which it was separated from its parent mass. Crystalline stones, such as quartz, are symmetrically angular, and those angles are based on the underlying molecular structure. Sandstone, shales, and some basalts (in particular columnar basalts) can have very sharp and precise angles created by compression and/or obstruction; essentially, these stones were molded into a pattern reflective of their confinement.

Angular stones are among the easiest to work with because their surface planes easily allow the creation of implied planes, and are thus very useful in creating continuity of form and melding together the components of the arrangement. Most stone groupings call for a broad spectrum of sizes, which is generally not a problem to find with this type of stone as it is common to most areas. You can also fit angular stones together to create interesting formations that appear to be fissures and cracks within a larger body of stone. In addition, these stones work well as bracing or shimming pieces because the angles provide solid support below the exposed surface.

Notice how the angular stones used to make this waterfall ▶ create the illusion that they belong to a single larger body of stone filled with fissures and cracks.

Embedded Elements

Stones are often amalgams of different media that have been fused into a single object. The juxtaposition of these elements can create context among multiple stones in a grouping, adding considerable interest to a stone group's appearance. The three major types of embedded elements are fissures, concretions, and inclusions.

Fissures

Fissures are naturally occurring fractures in a rock's surface. Although fissures are not actually physical elements fused into the parent stone, we consider them to be examples of embedded elements because from a visual standpoint, the positive space of the stone contains the negative space of the fissure. They are wonderful to work with because you can create a great sense of energy or movement by aligning the fractures to give broad hints at what the motivation of a stone composition could be. They also create obvious lines that you can emphasize as you create your grouping. They add a certain depth to the stone itself, but even more important, you can visually tie your stones together with these lines. Try aligning smaller stones with the planes and lines established by the fault and fracture lines for a singularly unique creation. Fissured stones can be especially effective used with plants, which will add to the illusion of great antiquity in your stone display.

Angles of the distinctive lines in fissures can be repeated through your composition to build a great sense of continuity and internal context.

◄ Fissures can take on massive proportions, such as this one in Hocking Hills, Ohio.

Concretions

Concretions are usually found in sandstone as dense fluid folds of the stone embedded into itself. They are of a slightly different texture and are more resistant to wear and erosion than the bulk of the stone's surface. Concretions can be a challenge to use as an integrating element, but when you can line up the right combination and arrangements, the result is quite dramatic.

Concretions form beautiful ribbon-like patterns in the very surface of the stones.

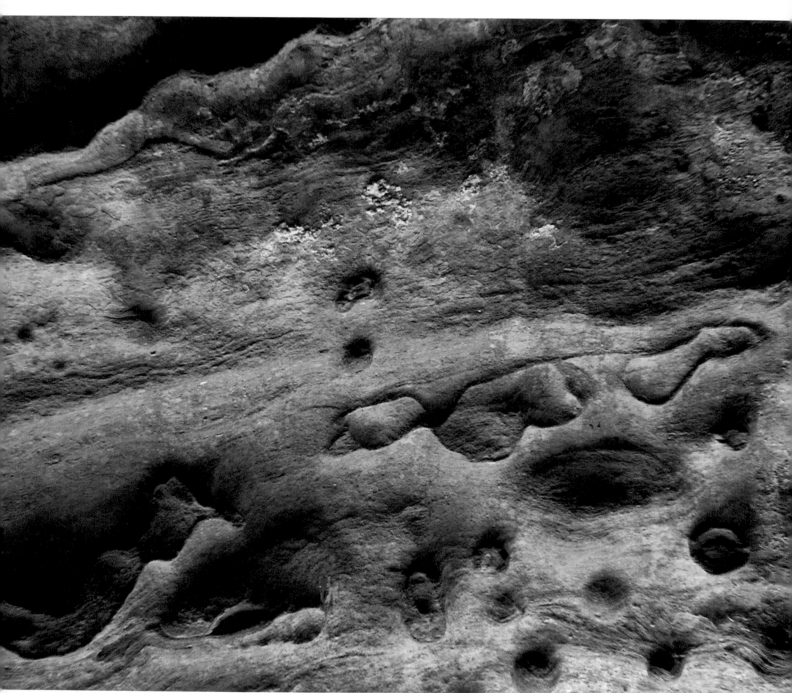

Inclusions

Inclusions are embedded lines of a different type of stone within a rock you are using. As a general rule, inclusions are white in color, but this can vary considerably by region. The width of the bands can also vary significantly. Stones with inclusions can provide a basis or focal point for an entire grouping; you can also use inclusions to create unifying lines of force within the stone group. In time you can learn to create a composition within a composition: Have the outer whole of your grouping make a different statement than the unified whole buried within. For instance, you may have a stone grouping whose outward motivation is an eroding mountain range; the alignment of the inclusions within the stones, however, creates a wave of white lines that runs at counterpoint to the rhythm of the false mountain.

Inclusions can range from small white lines threading their way across the surface of a single stone (left) to huge stripes of color running through a massive geological formation (right).

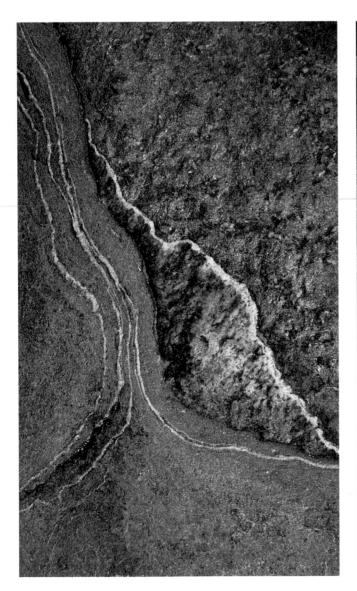

Married Stone

This stone is, in essence, a variation on stone with inclusions. Rather than being embedded, the contrasting stones are joined together as though welded. Married stone is very unusual and difficult to find — it is usually serendipity or accident that will bring this type of stone to a project. Married stone can lend itself to such themes as duality and yin-yang, but even more interesting is the different ways the stones will have weathered while attached. You can often find fantastic shapes. In one such case, a married stone appeared to be a mother holding her child; in another, there appeared a series of what looked like snowcapped peaks.

Artificial Stones

Two summers ago, we designed and installed a rooftop garden for a local television station. The president-owner had a perfect spot on his building for such a garden; the second-floor lobby and many of the offices would benefit from it. With a structural engineer, we put together the reinforcement and waterproof membrane needed to make our design come to fruition. But that design called for a number of boulders, and a few calculations told us that one of the necessary stones was just too heavy for our rooftop. We had to find an alternate — not a different design, just a lighter stone. The answer came from modern technology: an artificial stone. This stone had to be more realistic than the boulders Superman used to throw around because the garden was going to be scrutinized at close range by hundreds of people every day.

Artificial stones are obviously not something you find in nature; they're molded and created according to the needs of the situation. During the Victorian era, huge artificial boulders were often constructed on elaborate armatures and frameworks. This made moving and placing the stones considerably easier. Today, injection molding of templates taken directly from the field have created relatively light "stones" made of polymers or stone dust and cement that, when dyed, are convincingly stonelike in appearance. (The artificial stone described above can be seen in the far right corner of the photograph of the rooftop garden featured on page 10.)

Exceptionally rare in nature, married stone is the joining of two or more different types of stone into one solid piece, as if they were welded together.

BASIC MORPHOLOGICAL CHARACTERISTICS

In order to effectively create beautiful stone arrangements from the various types of stone, you also need to think of stone's basic forms. Success in the sculptural aspects of your creation lies in putting together the right forms in an appropriate arrangement. In some groupings, you will use for the most part only one basic form; in others, you'll use all of the basic forms. The four primary categories of form in stone are horizontal, chunky, vertical, and arcing.

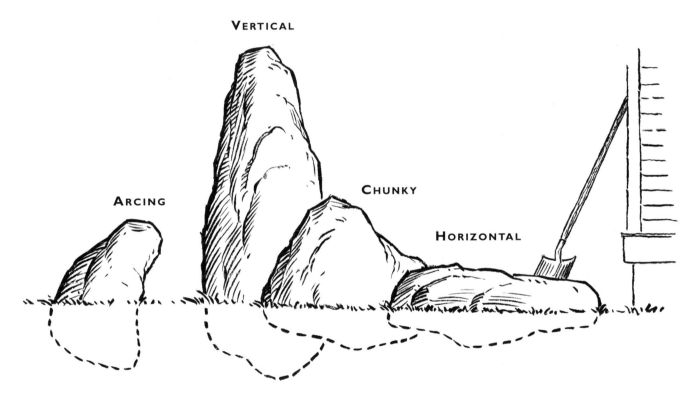

Horizontal

Horizontal stones fall into two groups: low and high. *Low* horizontal stones help give a base to an arrangement, and are often used to create depth by placing them as part of the foreground. *High* horizontal stones can be used similarly to chunky stones — as an integrating element. They can also be used in hillside arrangements that mimic cliff faces. When spread throughout an entire landscape, they can provide a subtle underlying internal context that unifies the composition. Low horizontal stones normally have a ratio of height to width of 1:3 or 1:2.

These chunky stones have been used as steps leading up to a wooden deck — informal steps over a moat up to the rampart. Seen from afar, the stones could be used to frame and establish the foreground or background of a stone composition set in front of or behind them.

Chunky

Blocky, somewhat angular stones fall into the chunky category. They are usually uniform in girth and the ratio of height to width is about 2:3. Their role within a group is usually one of helping consolidate the entire arrangement. The viewer's eye is led through the arrangement by the subtle placement of the implied planes you have created through these stones. Sometimes this form of stone will be used as a foreground or midground element to create a greater sense of depth in the grouping.

Vertical

Stones that have a primarily upright character can be called vertical. Such stones are either relatively flat or fairly uniform in girth. Although not fixed, the ratio of height to width is usually about 3:1. The portion of each stone that is normally placed in the ground is its widest part, with the tapered portion pointing skyward. Most often, the top of the stone is not directly in the center but rather off to one side. In many types of arrangements this is the first stone to be placed, thereby helping establish the dispersal and placement of the remaining stones in the group. Vertical stones also make good focal points.

This unusual vertical stone set in a Japanese-style garden draws the attention of the viewer to the garden's edge. It helps to enhance a sense of space with its own great size and by drawing the viewer's eye to the meandering path that runs next to it and leads beyond the viewer's sight.

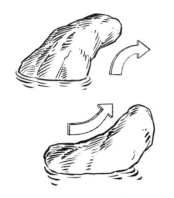

Arcing stones are useful tools for directing the viewer's eye toward a focal point.

Arcing

Arcing stones are more unusual than the other three types, but can be very effective if used appropriately in an arrangement. They are most commonly used as a device for leading the eye within the group of stones, or for leading it from outside the arrangement to an inside focal point. In the latter application, the focal point is the natural end path in the eye's journey through the placed stones — the view you really want the observer to look at. Occasionally, you'll have the opportunity to use a multitude of arcing stones in a group. This makes for a very dramatic composition. Ratios vary widely, depending on the stone and the circumstances in which it will be used.

TOTAL VOLUME OF STONES NEEDED

A large factor to consider when you go looking for stone is exactly how much stone you will need for your project. If you need a truckload of stone, for instance, and all you can find of a particular type is a wheelbarrow's worth, you are going to have to adjust your composition or find another source. It is always possible to go back and add stones later, but we do not recommend this. It will disturb the plants and be much more expensive. It is far better to be sure that you have enough stones to accomplish your task to begin with. In most cases, you should have at least a third more stones on hand than you need. In this way, you will have plenty to choose from and not have to work with whatever is left over.

If you are in the fortunate position of having all the stones you need on hand, you may have a different problem: compromising your design because you want to use something that already exists, even if it is not the very best stone for your plans. The bottom line with stone on site is that it will determine the nature of the composition you build. At times, this can be a creative challenge; at other times, it is just a frustrating dead end filled with compromises. You have to be the final judge in this situation.

Malleability of the Site

Here's one final consideration in your choice of stones: How forgiving is the surface in which you'll be placing these stones? If you have shallow soil over a ledge environment, you may need to look for stones with relatively flat bases. If you cannot bury your stones because of shallow soil, you also have the choice of cutting them along their base lines just below where you know the soil or plant line will be. Another option may be to build up the area with berms or mounds, or even to raise the grade of the entire environment. (For more discussion of this topic, see page 28.)

FINDING STONES

"Water, water everywhere and not a drop to drink," goes *The Rime of the Ancient Mariner,* but when it comes to finding stones for the landscape, *The Ode to the Stone Mason* might read, "Stone, stone everywhere but not a rock to keep!" The very earth we walk on is stone to its core, and yet trying to find good stones to use in the landscape can be frustrating. In this chapter we will not only tell you where to find stones you can keep but also give you some hints that will make your experiences less painful. You will learn stone-collecting etiquette and how to avoid being shot at by an angry landowner.

There is a growing need to find stones. Designers, architects, homeowners, businesses, and even municipalities are using stones for rock and specialty gardens, walls, water features, sculpture, and textural accents. Other cultures have long known of the beauty of stone in the landscape, and have made stone acquisition a big business. Here in North America, the need for stones has brought forth a whole new industry over the last 20 years, and made the right stone for the job at hand a valuable commodity. Farmers and landowners have found that many of the interior fieldstone walls and boulders on their properties have a new and unexpected value. If you have stones on your property, don't give them away. Get an idea what they're worth. To the rest of you who want stones and don't have them, we dedicate this chapter.

Stones can be found on private, commercial, and public land. Unfortunately, you cannot just go out and grab stones willy-nilly throughout the countryside. There are rules of etiquette you must follow, not to mention laws of trespass and ownership. You might think that because you pay taxes to the federal government, you should be able to go out and pick up any rock you want off public land. Not so! Your neighbors and their neighbors' neighbors pay taxes, too, and they have the right to see those same rocks that you want to cart off.

You may also think, "Well, it's only a rock. What would be the harm in taking it?" The problem is that this rock has a quantifiable value, and while people may not have been aware of this fact a few years ago, they've now caught on. Just look at the popularity of stone nurseries across the country.

Still, when stones are the quarry (no pun intended), there are many avenues for you to pursue. Keep in mind that you might find rocks in various places, such as abandoned or dilapidated buildings, not specifically covered in this chapter. Be original in your approach, keep your eyes open for opportunity, and then seize the moment. You'll be glad you did.

Where Stone Hides

When I was a young man in 1973, I purchased my first home. It was in a coastal town in one of "those new developments." I was understandably excited with the prospect of landscaping my "moonscape" yard. One of the items first on my list was to establish a permanent boundary between my neighbor and my three-quarter acre lot. I was young and in need of establishing my place in the world, and since I lived in New England and more specifically Maine, I thought, "A stone wall is what I need."

An immediate problem was where to find stone for such a wall. The stone normally used for walls was picked off the land when our forebears were clearing farmland from out of the woods. All I had was 4 inches (10 cm) of loam on top of a clay-sand mix used to backfill all around my house. There were also some cannon-ball-size stones that had migrated to the surface through the last 40 years, when my property had stood fallow.

It has been accepted lore in New England for years that the glaciers brought the millions of stones that the settlers found strewn everywhere. When asked where the glaciers went, the inevitable Yankee reply is "Back for more stones."

In the North, people are painfully aware of the freeze-thaw cycle, because it tends to pull stones upward to the surface. A theory put forward by John Jerome in his book Stone Work is that when the ground freezes tightly around the tough, hard upper surface of a stone, then heaves upward, this actually pulls the stone toward the ground's surface until it eventually shows up in some innocent's lawn or garden.

If I had to wait for this process or for the glaciers' return to gain enough stones for my dream boundary wall, however, I would be finishing my wall sometime around 2110. I had to come up with an alternative and less time-consuming method of acquiring my stones.

The plan I came up with was simple: Drive around until I found a wall with stones I liked, find out who owned it, purchase the stones, and move them back to my house to build the wall. But simple seems to be a word used only by people describing the "Simon meeting the Pieman" or young, slightly naive people such as myself.

I decided to take a Sunday drive to accomplish my first objective. This was easily done. After church, a friend and I pointed my Pinto wagon inland, heading for the hills and walls of western Maine. We knew that finding a farmer's wall, which seemed to be doing nothing other than slowly falling over, was our best bet.

Our drive was quickly rewarded by a plethora of walls. It seems that at the turn of the century in rural Maine, every square inch (cm) of available land was being used in some farming capacity. After only cruising for about a half hour, we landed in a small town called New Gloucester. Here was a veritable table of plenty for stone picking. On a secluded, sparsely populated, tree-covered, wall-lined country road we found the perfect stone wall. It sat close to the road for easy access, and it seemed to be tall and wide enough that only a small percentage of its stones would be enough to build my small boundary wall — and this wall would never know I'd been there.

The "larceny in the night" side of me said, "Go ahead, just take what you need, no one will ever know." The right thing to do, though, of course, was find the owner and offer him or her money for the stone. I knocked on the door of the first farmhouse I found.

"Let me get this straight, son." The farmer, Malcolm, stood behind his slightly rusted screen door. "You want to give me money for stones that not only I've been tossing off my fields for years, but my dad and his dad have as well?" The man thought he had an absolute lunatic on his hands. "Alma, would you come here a minute," he called toward an open door leading down a dark hallway. As the four of us stood out on his paint-peeling porch that spring morning, hammering out the details of what stone was worth, I knew I'd hit on something. I just wasn't sure what.

We finally agreed on the price after a cup of tea. I settled into my Pinto wagon's almost-cloth seat recalling our conversation. "You going to haul it with that wagon?" Malcolm had asked. I knew that by the time I had completed this wall, many people in that small town would know about the young man in the orange Pinto wagon who paid good money to break his back.

— Frederick Campbell

Stone Walls

Traveling around the countryside will reveal a rich source of weathered stones: construction of old. Our forebears not only brought forth a new nation, they left us tens of thousands of miles of stone walls. These walls were often used for boundaries, but at other times, in the settlers' urgent need for tillable land, they simply piled the stones dug up from the fields. Amazingly enough, even in a two-hundred-year-old wall, only the stones that are directly exposed will have a weathered appearance. Depending on how tightly or closely stacked the wall was, the stones in the interior will often be as white or brown as the day they were placed there. If you're looking for weathered stone, you may need to pass up these interior stones, or be prepared to let them sit for a year or so.

Finding these walls, boulders, and stone piles may be as easy as taking a trip to the country, but you'll often need to do some research, because the best walls are frequently invisible from public roads. A good resource is the town or city hall's tax records. Most towns have aerial photos of properties. These photos are your eyes in the sky for locating your stone bonanzas.

Private Land

There are many sources of stones on private land. However, there are also some important standards of etiquette that you must be aware of before venturing out into the countryside on a stone-collecting mission:

1. Don't trespass. Ask the landowners for permission to explore the property.
2. Communicate with the landowners. Share with them what you are doing. The more they know, the more apt they are to let you onto their property. They may even offer help, in the form of a tractor.
3. Leave the site in better shape than you found it. For example, repair your ruts.
4. Never take more than you need.
5. Do not mark stone with spray paint; use chalk or a removable marker, such as a ribbon.
6. Get permission to remove any trees or bushes that may have grown up into the harvest area.
7. Be careful not to remove stones that could initiate or exacerbate an erosion problem.
8. Pay a fair price for the stones. This will vary by region and stone availability. You can find out what's a fair price by checking in with a local stone center, pit, or *stone broker* (a person who buys stone for redistribution to masons, stone centers, and landscape contractors).

New Construction Sites

Construction sites are also a good source of stones. Frequently, road construction crews must blast through veins of stone. This can be a veritable godsend to the stone enthusiast. Here again, though, you'll need permission and perhaps a company to work with to secure your stones. The best way to find them is to go to town or city hall and look for the permits that have been issued. Newspapers often list these permits in their classified sections, as well.

If you're building a home, you may find that blasting is needed to put in a foundation. This happens more frequently than you might imagine, and although it might seem to be a hardship in the home-construction phase of your project, you can cash in on it in two ways: once with stone selection for your own landscape, and twice by selling stones to other interested collectors.

While blasting on your future homesite is going on, it is wise for you to make your stone selections right away, saving the best and allowing the excavation crew to remove the slag. (Junk rocks are good only for fill.) Our clients frequently have us work with excavation folks to make these selections.

Old Foundations

Old abandoned homesteads are often good sources of stones. If you are lucky enough to locate such a site and the landowner, bank, or town agrees that you can have stones from it, you could end up with some of the finest cut and natural stones available. We have found old foundations to be one of the more expensive sources because of access, but for us stone junkies no price is too steep for these gems.

Frequently, you'll have to pull stones from an old foundation set deep in the ground, or cut a new road to the abandoned site. Although these things can cost you in time and money — since most folks don't own a backhoe for lifting, let alone a trailer large enough to haul the stones once they've been located and excavated — your effort may be rewarded. Even to the most discerning eye, old foundations yield some beautifully aged, top-rated cut stones.

Finding these old foundations is a challenge. Again, looking in town tax records is a great way to see where old homesteads may have once been located. This may also be a time to see if there is an older local historian about, one who would love nothing better than to be taken to lunch and asked questions about the town in "the old days." If no such person can be found, most towns have historical societies in need of a donation; they can provide loads of information on this subject.

Finding Weathered Stone

Many people are looking for weathered, moss-covered stones for projects. If you can't find any don't worry — a few years of exposure to the weather will have the desired effect on your stones. There are also ways to speed this process up, such as brushing buttermilk or manure tea on your stones, which will encourage lichen and moss to grow there.

You may encounter problems if you place mossy stones in full sun. In just a short time, that special lichened or mossy effect is lost — the sun kills it. Thus, it is particularly important to know the conditions in which you are placing mossy stones. If you are fortunate to have a water source such as irrigation or a stream close by, you can keep many mosses growing by not letting them dry out.

Broken Dams

Wherever waterwheels were used to power commerce of any kind, you may find fallen-down stone dams. Many farms once boasted hydropower, as did many municipalities. Here again old tax records as well as historical and human resources are good sources of information. These old sites are often located on privately owned land. If you are looking for cut stones with weather and water erosion, you may find what you're after at these old dams. The biggest caveat is these sites may also be of some historical significance; you will need to proceed with care and respect. Do your research and make doubly sure that you're legally free to remove stones from the site. Don't become a stone bandit.

Abandoned Quarries

Abandoned mines or quarries are often an overlooked resource that could be an oasis of stones for many uses in the landscape. First and foremost, though, you must find these quarries. Sometimes local tax maps and town records will show you their locations. The state may have a record of all registered quarries and mines, both active and inactive. You may also be able to get this information by calling the Department of Environmental Protection. You could also try calling the geological survey department for your state. In addition, the Internet has hundreds of web sites with information, including that of the United States Geological Survey (www.usgs.gov).

Obsolete Bridges

In older communities, in addition to old dams, you can often find abandoned stone bridge abutments — huge monoliths of massed stone standing on either side of the water's edge, facing each other across the moving water, the bridge between them long ago removed or fallen and swept downstream. You can sometimes see them just a few feet down the river from modern roadways as they cross the water on new steel bridges; then again, you can sometimes also find them along old, abandoned railway routes. If you are lucky enough to find one, these bridge abutments are excellent sources of waterworn cut stone. These sites are often public property and may be of historical significance, so make sure that you obtain permission from the proper authorities before removing any stone. You'll probably need large equipment to dismantle one of these old bridges (and we highly recommend working with a professional crew), but the quality and size of the stones may make it worth your trouble.

Commerce Meets the Stone

Many of you may be reading this and thinking, "I don't have time to scour the country for stones, let alone hiring construction crews or lugging stones around. Even if I weren't committed, there would be a lot of talk at the local dump." And we would agree with you — we don't always have time, either. Fortunately, as stones have grown steadily in popularity as landscaping features, commerce in them has increased to match. There are even some stone centers that will ship stone to your worksite (see the appendix).

Stone Centers

There is a relatively new resource for the stone-searching public — the stone nursery. Similar to garden nurseries, stone nurseries stock many different varieties of stone. In fact, with the increasing popularity of stonescaping, many garden nurseries are developing stone nurseries right on their premises. And these stone nurseries deliver, which could eliminate one problem aspect of your stone project: You won't have to find a truck. Many of these businesses also have delivery trucks equipped with a small crane for offloading, and will only charge an hourly fee to help you place your stones. This can be a great time saver.

Stone centers typically focus on paving and wall stones, although over the past few years, in response to the growing interest in natural stonescapes, they have started to stock larger boulders and accent stones. In Japan, most garden centers have separate stone centers.

These stores primarily carry varieties of paving and wall stone. If you are planning a waterfall, stream, or pond, however, they also offer products such as bluestone, flat fieldstone, cobblestone, and limestone. And although this was once unusual, stone centers now often have available accent stones and boulders you can use for stone compositions. Such stones are also useful in water features.

Landscape Contractors and Stone Brokers

Many people use their local landscape or stonemason contractors as their stone providers. Landscape contractors and masons will also be able to deliver and place your stones for you. They often have their own supplies of stones and may even have a source for an indigenous stone that no one else has — if, for example, they have an exclusive deal with a farmer or *stone broker*. The latter is a middleman who has worked out deals with local landowners for stones he or she sells only in the local market. Using professional contractors is a good idea, but you should check their portfolios as well as references.

Quarries and Gravel Pits

It seems that every town has a gravel pit, and if you're willing, this may be your final low-cost stone option. Many pits are in the business or practice of putting their larger stones in a pile to be crushed later. You can often purchase these stones inexpensively. One big catch is that they have just been unearthed, and you'll have to wait until nature can take its course for the beauty of weathered stones.

Many gravel and crushed-stone operations blast stones in their quarries. The best time to find stones for your projects is just after these "blasts." You must get permission to enter these places for liability reasons — and if you don't have the right insurance, you may not be able to get permission. Often masons or landscape professionals have already made arrangements to select and pick up stones. In our case, for example, we have made agreements with many of our local pits and quarries. This enables us to take customers, including landscape architects, into these stone supermarkets and do a little shopping.

Artificial Stones

Several businesses around the country and world manufacture artificial stones from various synthetic and lightweight materials, and they look very realistic. Check the listings in your phone book under "Stone Suppliers," or check the Internet for these companies.

Part of the problem with artificial stones is the limited availability of specific textures, shapes, and forms that would help you put together

Buying from a Vendor

Stones obtained from a commercial vendor can come from anywhere in the country. The structures, forms, and colors of your stones are going to vary according to the inherent and underlying geology of the region from which they were taken. For example, eastern Pennsylvania fieldstone is gray and blocky or round. Western stone tends to be round, with brown or red hues. In the Northeast, quarried stones tend toward white, pink, and blue-gray colors.

artistic creations. Usually you'll find that only a fixed selection of forms has been produced by the manufacturer. Rather than dealing with off-the-shelf artificial stone, then, you may need to find an artificial stone manufacturer who can work personally with you to design and build your arrangement from scratch. This person, as well as you, will require a keen eye and understanding of not only natural forms, but also the appropriate aesthetic principles for placing those forms in a way that elicits an emotional response in the viewer.

Public Land

The public domain includes large tracts of land owned and managed by federal, state, county, and local governments. When it comes to stone gathering, the good thing is that this land belongs to us all, and the bad thing is that this land belongs to us all. When you hike through the parks, you can't help but notice some great stones — but you'd better leave them unless you have permission to remove them. How, then, can such places become potential stone-harvesting sites? The answer lies in the use of the land. Parkland, no matter what branch of government manages it, may host projects from time to time that require removal or blasting of stones. If you contact the park services in your area and let these folks know what you're after, you may succeed.

Public rights-of-way are another resource you could use for stone gathering. When a public road is being built or expanded, construction may include blasting or the removal of ledge. Often the site excavator is looking for places to haul this "junk stone." If you are in the right place at the right time, you may be the benefactor of good stones at no cost. Many towns have what are called "paper roads" — rights-of-way under construction that are owned by the town but not yet converted to pavement. Just keep your eyes open for construction while you drive about — it is an infrequent source of stone wealth, but you can never leave any "stone unturned" in your quest.

Working with Stone 6

This chapter explores a number of tools and techniques you can use to make your stone-moving task easier (or should we say, to make the task doable, because *easy* and *moving stone* are simply not compatible terms). There are, no doubt, more ways not covered here. However, in our 50-some years of combined experience, and in our continuing quest for placing just the right stone in just the right place, we have tried almost all of these tools and methods. They work.

Working with stones by hand has its pleasures. There's nothing that compares with moving and maneuvering stones large and small using only your own sweat and ingenuity. However, to say that hydraulics is the best, fastest, easiest, and just plain safest way to move stones would be an understatement. It is true that the Great Pyramids, Stonehenge, and the castles of Europe, ancient Rome, and Greece were all built without the aid of modern machines. But in the 20th century we have an edge with our machines, and we use them every day.

One note we should make here is that when you are considering the tools you will need for your project, buy or rent quality, or hire professionals to do your work. If you buy cheap tools, your work will reflect that decision. If a tool breaks, particularly when you're out in the middle of East Overshoe, it's no fun having to leave the job to look for a new one.

However, we're not recommending that you go out and buy lots of expensive tools if you are only moving and placing a few stones just this once. In many cases, you can rent all the tools you'll need, from wheelbarrows to tractors, from a local hardware or garden shop. If you haven't had much experience using motorized or hydraulic equipment, get someone to help you who has, or consider hiring a professional contractor or landscaper. Really huge boulders that require really big equipment are not out-of-the-question for the backyard stone enthusiast, but they'd best be left for an experienced person with the right equipment to move and place. Above all, watch out for your toes!

SAFETY FIRST

Quick Equipment Reference

- **Marking the layout:** Grade stakes, flags, surveyor's tape, tape measures, measuring wheels, string, fluorescent spray paint

- **Digging holes:** Backhoe, trackhoe, shovel, bulldozer

- **Moving stones:** Vehicle, crane, bobcat loader, bulldozer, tractor equipped with forks, stone sled, pipes, wheelbarrow, garden cart, ball-cart, come-along, winch, chain pull, block and tackle, tripod, cant dog, planking, chain, rope, nylon strapping, pry bars

- **Setting stones:** Backhoe, trackhoe, crane, bobcat loader, bulldozer, tractor with buckets or forks, block and tackle, tripod, cant dog, planking

- **Backfilling:** Backhoe, bulldozer, shovel

- **Measuring lines and angles:** Plumb bob, level, theodolite, transist

- **Adjusting set stones:** Bulldozer, planking, pry bar, bracing, shim stones, crane, pipes, come-along, winch, chain pull, block and tackle, tripod, cant dog

The one unifying element in all construction — from stone gathering to placement and everything in between — is the need for safety. Thinking ahead and knowing the best techniques for construction are important, but before you consider any of that, there are basic rules of safety and respect for the materials and people you are working with that you should know and obey.

Whether you are picking stones in the woods, on an abandoned homestead, at a construction site, or even in the fields, be careful. Piles of stones are subject to sudden shifting. You may already know to watch for it in a quarry or on a construction site, but remember that you also need to be careful in old foundations and around old walls. It's not uncommon for the removal of one stone to result in tons of others moving suddenly and without warning.

When you are working with stones, we recommend that you wear the following:

- **Hard hat.** Protect your head!

- **Gloves.** A good pair of gloves can save your hands from scrapes. Wear gloves that fit snugly to help you with grasp and feel — your hand can easily slip out of a loose glove when carrying a heavy stone. We suggest gloves of deerskin or leather; cloth gloves just won't survive the wear and tear. Some masons use only adhesive tape on their fingertips, to save the skin there, so that they can still feel a stone with the rest of their hand.

- **Sturdy footwear.** Do *not* go about lifting and moving heavy rocks barefoot or in sneakers — you're liable to cut your feet on sharp rock or even drop a stone on yourself and break a toe! Some folks use steel-toed boots when they are working with stones. They're not a bad idea for toe protection, but they're certainly no guarantee that the top of your foot or your leg won't be attacked by an errant stone. Whatever you choose, make sure it's sturdy — bare feet or sneakers are *bad* ideas.

- **Safety goggles.** Never chip or smash a stone without a pair of safety goggles. Even with glasses on, a stone shard may fly into the unprotected side. We've seen a chipped piece of granite pop off and embed itself into a mason's leg, right though his jeans. Imagine if it had been his eye!

PREPARING THE WORKSITE

Once you have a rough idea of where your stonescape will be, you need to do some initial site preparation. The first order of business is to mark off the area, including any off-limit boundaries, proposed planting sites, and, if you'll be building around a particular focal stone, the spot where the focal stone will be placed. We frequently use orange spray paint or surveyor's tape for this. You can do this before or after the stone is delivered — just be sure that the stone is not dumped on the spot where you'll be building.

Before you get going, make sure that you've examined soil conditions. If you're going to need to institute drainage (see page 108), you may need to prepare for that now.

Marking the Layout

Once the stone is delivered, start selecting the tops and bottoms (which part will be seen, and which part will be buried). Measure the bottom of the stone, both circumference and height, and make note of it so you'll know what size hole to dig for it. Keep in mind that most stones need to have at least one-third of their mass in the ground. In many instances you will bury more than one-third of the stone, but rarely less.

If you have roughed out a design, now is the time to refine it. If you haven't, now may be the time to sketch one. Choose one stable on-site fixture — such as the first stone placed, a hedge, or a tree — and use that as your *benchmark,* the standard from which all other placements or elevations will be measured. It's easiest to draft a plan on graph paper scaled to one-quarter (one side of every square on the plan equals 4 feet [m] on the site) or one-eighth (one side of every square equals 8 feet [m]). However you choose to reduce the scale, be consistent throughout. (For a step-by-step list of the design principles to consider when sketching a plan, see page 26.)

If you're going to place stones on a grade or hillside, you'll need to take the elevation of that spot in order to know how high the stone placed there will be in comparison with your benchmark and, later on, the other stones in the composition. Measure how high or low it is in comparison to your benchmark (or a spot on your benchmark). If it's not too far, you can measure by stretching a string with a line level (see page 112) from the benchmark to the slope (to establish a level plane), and then measure up or down with a 4-foot (1.2 m) level (see page 111) and a tape measure. Note these elevations on your plan.

Although there are certainly more scientific methods, you can rough out elevations with simply a few basic tools.

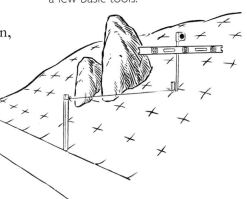

Transfer your design from paper to landscape with grade stakes or flags.

With a rough plan in hand, mark the proposed site for each stone with a grade stake or flag. If the elevation is important, you can mark the proposed above ground height of the stone on a grade stake to help you as you dig a hole and then set the stone. Doing this preliminary layout work gives you the opportunity to view your future work without having to move and remove stones. Keep in mind that a plan is rarely followed to the letter, and you will most likely propose many changes as you progress through the placement of your design. We politely call these "on-site modifications."

Grade Stakes

You can purchase grade stakes in a variety of lengths at most lumberyards in bundles of twenty-five or more. We find the 4-foot (1.2 m) length to be most useful. Grade stakes are sharpened on one end, and they can be used for marking stone locations or layout and grade elevations. They're made from a variety of woods; hardwood stakes, if you can find them, hold up best to being repeatedly pounded into the ground.

Flags

You can buy the flags used for layout at a surveyor's supply shop. They come in high-visibility colors, such as fluorescent orange, pink, or yellow. The flag is attached to a thick, heavy-mil wire that comes in different lengths and will stand upright in the ground. The advantage flags have over grade stakes is their brightness — they're easier to see and can be more useful for marking placement, especially if you're working in a large site. They are also used for just one purpose — layout — and won't be confused for any other, such as grade stakes marking elevations. You can also write on them with a permanent marker, identifying whatever it is that they're marking, to further eliminate any confusion with layout.

Surveyor's Tape

Surveyor's tape is traditionally used by surveyors to mark boundaries and pin locations. It comes in rolls in a wide variety of high-visibility colors. You can wrap it around grade stakes to make them more visible or anchor it with a nail on the ground to mark layout. Surveyor's tape can also be wrapped around a stone to designate it for future pickup without leaving any permanent marks.

Tape Measures

Tape measures, used for measuring everything from elevations to distances between stones, are a necessity for layout. We have two favorites:

String

String could be the most versatile and cost-effective tools in your mason and design bag. When you add a couple of other inexpensive tools, such as plumb bobs and line levels (see page 112), there is no question about its usefulness. If your project is a streambed or a waterfall feature, you can pin string to the ground or tie it between grade stakes to mark the *banking*, the edges of the water flow. It can also be used for marking the radius of pools or backwash. String is useful for making a straight line and, lacking a tape measure, can also help you measure relative distances.

We like to use a high-quality woven cloth string. You can also buy a reel, sold separately, to keep the string tangle-free.

a shorter, 25-foot (7.6 m) metal tape measure, and a longer cloth tape measure. The metal tape won't stretch, and gives an accurate reading even when it's years old. The drawback is that it can tear or snap out of its case, especially when used for longer measurements. Speaking from personal experience, consider your 25-foot measure to be a 20-foot (6.1 m) measure — it will last longer! Many people in the construction field use a longer cloth tape measure for measurements over 25 feet (7.6 m), as it's less likely to break. Longer tape measures (of cloth or metal, whichever you decide upon) come on a spool with a handle for quick retrieval, while the shorter metal tapes have a spring-loaded case.

Digging Holes

As mentioned many times before, for stability and a sense of naturalness, you'll want at least one-third of the stone set in the ground. Measure the bottom of the stone, criss-crossing in at least two and preferably more directions, and then mark the circumference of the hole on the ground with spray paint or surveyor's tape. If you're digging a large hole, you may need to use a backhoe or trackhoe. You can dig smaller holes with a shovel.

You may want to dig the hole a little wider than necessary, as you can always backfill (see page 110) around it. However, be careful not to dig a hole that's too deep, as then you'll have to remove the stone from the hole — not an easy task — in order to backfill and raise up the bottom.

Backhoes and Trackhoes

Most people have seen a backhoe and know that it looks like a tractor with a front-end bucket loader, a hydraulic shovel on the rear, and pneumatic tires. The trackhoe is like a big backhoe without the loading bucket; it also has metal treads like a tank. Many trackhoes have buckets that can scoop 1, 2, or even 3 yards (m) at a time.

With a backhoe and a trackhoe, you can prepare the site by digging holes, if needed, for placing the stones. However, they are also useful for setting stone and backfilling. If you can outfit your backhoe with a fork, like a forklift, instead of the front-end loader bucket, you can slide the fork under large stones for easy lifting and setting. With a trackhoe, a good operator can cradle a large stone in the shovel bucket and set it down exactly where you want it. It's a little more difficult to adjust if the operator doesn't get it quite right, however, since you can't spin the stone while it's in the bucket. If it's not quite right, we recommend that you leave the stone on the ground and use the trackhoe to push it around until it settles where you want it. You may need to blanket the edge of the trackhoe shovel to keep it from scraping the stone.

Measuring Wheels

Measuring wheels are another good way to make longer measurements, and they are less cumbersome than tape measures. Most come with a reset button on the counter and a retractable handle. The larger the wheel, the more accurate the measure, but also the more expensive the tool. Many designers and estimators are now using these wheels.

Shovels

Both rounded, pointed shovels and square, flat-bottomed shovels are very useful in digging holes to prepare for final placement of the stones. Even when a large hole for a large stone is dug by a backhoe or other piece of motorized equipment, you'll use a shovel to finish off the hole's bottom so that it more closely aligns with the form of the rock's bottom. You can also use shovels for backfilling.

MOVING STONES TO AND AROUND YOUR WORKSITE

One of the tricks in building a stone grouping is getting the stones to where you are going to use them. Whether you're transporting them from two towns over or simply moving them from the pile left by the bulk delivery truck, you'll need proper equipment. The stones you are working with can range from small and manageable to enormous and unbudgeable, and although there is a certain satisfaction in using simply your own strength, there's also something to be said for the time and energy saved by using a motorized piece of equipment! In any case, using the correct techniques and the right equipment to get the job done is of critical importance. You have spent a great deal of time and effort finding just the right stone for your site; now let's get it there in one piece and safely.

Moving and Maneuvering Large Boulders

If your stone grouping contains even one very large stone, you may want to consider renting or hiring an operator of apiece of heavy-duty motorized equipment. For the novice stone-mover, large and heavy boulders can be extremely tricky and downright dangerous. Caution is the order of the day. Always be sure your load is secure, but never trust that it is.

Bulldozers

Bulldozers are helpful but have some limitations. Their best applications are scooping ponds in clay soils and pushing boulders into place. If you are working on a site still in the preliminary stages of construction, a large dozer can push and spin your stones into place with ease. However, fine-tuning a stone's placement with a dozer requires finesse and patience. Good operators may be up to the fussy nature of the task, but you may want to consider using pry bars, a come-along, a winch, or a block and tackle, which are all easier to control, instead. Be warned that bulldozers tend to leave a churned-earth trail behind them, although you can easily fix this rut by regrading.

Vehicles

Helpful tools of transport can include station wagons, cars, and jeeps with trailers as well as trucks of all sizes and shapes. If you are loading a vehicle or trailer, you may be tempted to overload — resist it! An overloaded vehicle is unpredictable, especially when traveling downhill. Overloading can also stress your vehicle's suspension. If you're still not convinced, the state police could have plenty to say about it should they catch you driving a dangerously overloaded vehicle. In some states, a fine and/or a tow and impounding are used to dissuade the would-be lawbreaker. That sure can make the landscape project get expensive!

Many trucks and four-wheel-drive, all-terrain vehicles and jeeps are equipped with power winches. Although the winches are meant to help you get unstuck, they can also be great for moving, lifting, and placing stubborn rocks.

In building *Ascension* (featured on page 9), architect Rick Anderson found a crane invaluable for lifting large boulders up to the hillside to form the banks of the fantasy waterfall.

Cranes

Perhaps the best machine for moving and placing large stones is the crane. A crane uses slings to carry each stone and place it gently on the ground. It can lift and transport stones over short distances and is extremely versatile. A good crane operator can gently set a stone on a dime, and depending on the size of the crane, you can place and spin not only small stones but also very large stones weighing many tons.

Bobcat Loader

Bobcat loaders come in many different sizes, so you can match the lifting capacity of the loader you choose with the stone you're working with. They have a set of forks as well as a front scooping bucket. They're used to carry stones to holes, then push them upright in the holes. (For a photograph of a bobcat loader, see page 131.) Using a bobcat loader can be tricky, however — once the stone is in the ground, it's there to stay. If you don't have much experience using one, save the bobcat loader for transportation and use a tripod for setting (see page 107).

Stone Sleds and Boats

This piece of equipment is more likely to be called a *sled* in the snowy regions of the world and a *boat* in warmer regions. The stone sled or boat is great for moving large stones short distances; instead of struggling to pick up a stone, you just flop it onto the sled.

Baskets and Cradles

When using a crane or just pulling a rope to move a stone, a basket or cradle is a handy tool. In the case of a crane, it's a necessity. These webbed slings are made of rope, chain, nylon strapping, or wire. A webbed basket will disperse the weight of a stone evenly and make a safe, stable support for it while it is suspended above who knows what — perhaps your house! Many of these slings have a quick coupling system in their bottoms so you can get the sling under the stone, then release it once you've gotten the stone into place. A local construction or crane company may be able to offer you some options for purchasing one.

A stone sled or boat

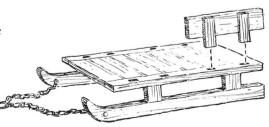

The sled or boat is usually constructed with two steel runners, has a hardwood bed such as oak, and has a chain connected to the front of its runners for pulling. We recommend that you don't use a model with a pull chain spot-welded to its runners. Instead, this chain should pass around the metal of the runner or be bolted all the way through the wood frame, as it will be less likely to pull out or snap under a heavy load than a spot weld. The best sleds are 12 inches (30 cm) or less off the ground. Some sleds have permanent sides, but many masons prefer a design that includes removable sides.

Pipes and Rollers

Pipes or log rollers can also be used to move large stones. Set a plank on the ground with one end resting on a couple of rollers. Roll a stone onto the plank, then push the plank and stone along atop the pipes or rollers. For best results, keep a minimum of three pipes under the stone-carrying board at all times. You will therefore need at least four pipes to do the job.

Planking and rollers are an efficient, low-tech system for moving large stones.

You can also roll a stone into place at a higher elevation with two planks. Start by placing the end of one plank on the higher spot, position the rollers on top, and then push the stone into place riding on the second board. Place a second, smaller, wedge-shaped rock between the stone and the last roller as a brake.

Moving and Maneuvering Smaller Stones

As you might imagine, smaller stones are easier to move and maneuver than large stones. That is not, however, an invitation to be less cautious. Working with our own hands and strength, without the aid of hydraulic equipment, is often more of a reason for us to take cover, not less.

Wheelbarrows

Wheelbarrows are quite useful for moving loads of smaller stones short distances. Keep in mind that many of us have regretted being impatient at one time or another, but rarely as immediately as when overloading a wheelbarrow. There's nothing quite so frustrating as accidentally dumping a wheelbarrow load of stones that took a good measure of time to fill — unless, of course, it's dumping it on yourself. So take your time

Moving a Full Load

Once you've loaded a sled with a heavy stone, be careful and don't get careless. A fully loaded sled can have a mind of its own. If you are on a slope, even a seemingly innocently pitched one, be prepared to move right along. The last thing you want is to get run over. This holds true for other forms of transport as well, including log rollers, pipes, carts, trailers, and the perennial favorite, the wheelbarrow. In all cases, don't overload. The stone will still be there for your next trip. Should your momentum get out of hand, you can bring along a wheel chuck or a 4 x 4 block of wood to throw in front of the runner as an emergency brake.

and don't overload! Place the majority of the weight over the handles, not the front end. This helps keep you from overloading it, because you will be lifting more of the weight, and gives you better control.

Wheelbarrows must be rugged and sturdily constructed. Get one that has solid oak handles, a real tire (preferably a filled one), and a steel belly or box.

Garden Carts

Garden carts can be a reliable way to move medium-size stones. They are quite easy to load; you simply flip the cart on its front end, push a stone onto the front piece of the cart, and then pull down the cart's handle. Voilà, your stone is ready for transport!

One caveat, though, is that garden carts are easy to overload because they are balanced so well. If the wheels scrape the top sides of the cart's sidewalls, the load is too heavy and you may have bent the axle on the cart. Unload the stone immediately before any more damage is done.

Ball-Carts

Ball-carts, designed for moving trees, are also excellent tools for moving stones. They generally have two wide, heavy-duty pneumatic tires placed on either side of the carrying cradle for stability, as well as long, upright handles for good leverage. A heavy duty, well-constructed ball-cart can handle as many stones as you can lug, so you should be careful not to load more than you can comfortably handle.

Below: A garden cart (bottom left), a wheelbarrow (bottom right), and ball-carts (top).

Come-Along, Winch, Chain Pull, and Block and Tackle

Come-alongs, winches, chain pulls, and block and tackles are tools normally hitched to a fixed point overhead and used to lift heavy objects. Auto mechanics often use them to lift engine blocks outside the confines of the car body. By applying the same principles and using a fixed point such as a tree or vehicle, you can move a large stone small distances with them. Each has its own advantages and disadvantages — you'll have to experiment to find out which tool you prefer.

Come-alongs, winches, chain pulls, and block and tackles take advantage of the laws of physics and make it possible to move large stones.

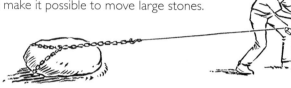

The **come-along** has two wheels wrapped in cable with a ratchet-type handle for pulling the cables in. To use it, hitch one end of cable to a fixed object, like a tree, and the other to your stone. Slowly turn the ratchet handle, pulling the stone toward the tree.

Winches are spools of cable powered by motor or a handle that locks with each turn. When mounted to a vehicle's frame, the motorized models are excellent for pulling a stone out of a hole or gully.

Chain pulls are engineered to alter the ratio between what is being lifted and the force the lifter is exerting, so that you can lift a weight that normally would be beyond your strength. A chain pull will lock and hold the object you are lifting and is best used with a tripod or a truck that has a tow crane.

The **block and tackle** has been around for years. Like the chain pull, it alters the ratio between what is being lifted and the lifter. You can change the rigging of a block and tackle by adding more blocks; this will enable you to hoist more weight. Experience with this tool is a must for correct use.

Planking

Planks are handy to keep around because they have a variety of uses. If you need to get a heavy stone to the top of a wall, you may simply want to flop or roll it up a plank you've rested on a wall or mound. If the stone in question is not too heavy, you can use a plank as a pry bar. In addition, you can place a stone on the end of a long plank and, by placing a fulcrum or pivot point under the middle of the plank, spin the plank, moving the stone into or closer to its desired resting place.

Tripods

Another great tool for moving, placing, and adjusting stones is the tripod, used with a block and tackle, chain-pull, come-along, or winch. It can be very helpful for lifting a large stone into a sled or boat. You can also use this invention in places no backhoe can go, and it can lift and move very heavy stones. Using the tripod to moves stones can be slow going because you must walk each stone step by step, lowering the stone so you can move the legs of the tripod and then raising the stone to shift it to the tripod's new position. Beams, poles, or pipes are used to make the legs, and a chain-pull winch provides the lift.

Tripods are particularly useful for setting stones, as they allow you to spin and adjust stones with little effort.

Cant Dog

A cant dog, used for moving logs, is also a good tool for moving stones. This tool has a hook and point attached to a 3- to 5-foot (.9 to 1.5 m) wooden handle. The hook has a flattened sharp end for grabbing and turning the rock over. Two people, each armed with a cant dog, can move a mountain of stones. Here, and whenever metal comes into direct contact with your stones, consider some padding to keep from scratching the stones.

Designed for moving logs, cant dogs are also useful tools for moving stones.

Dragging Stones

Whether you're moving a large or a small stone, you may at times wish to simply drag it across the ground with a tractor, a vehicle, or your own two feet to its appropriate spot. Although not the most sophisticated of methods, dragging is effective. In this case, you'll want to have a secure grasp of the boulder, chains, ropes, or nylon strapping before you begin pulling. Remember that dragging a stone will leave a rut in the ground proportionate to its size and weight.

Chain

A length of chain can come in handy for moving stones because it can help you get better leverage. Simply wrap the chain around the bottom of a stone, secure the end, and then pull. Chain is strong but heavy. It's most useful if your power source is a tractor or truck. When using chain, remember the old adage, "A chain is only as strong as its weakest link." Be sure to check it first for flaws.

Rope

A stout rope is always a great tool. The new hollow-core, woven, synthetic ropes are even stronger than the traditional hemp rope, and although they are more expensive, we consider the money well-spent.

Rigging rope for hauling a stone can be as complicated as weaving a net or basket or as simple as tying a loop around the rock. Many people weave a teardrop eyelet with a snap hook into the end of the rope. This makes attaching to and detaching from a stone much less time consuming. Any time you use a rope to pull a stone, be sure to tie a knot that will come undone when you're through, such as a bowline. That way you won't have to cut the rope off the rock.

Nylon Strapping

Nylon is both strong and tear resistant. As strapping, it comes in a variety of widths, and its strength is directly proportional to its width and thickness. For moving stones, it can be used like chain or rope. The advantage of using these straps is that unlike chain, they don't mark up the stones, and unlike rope, they don't stretch.

SETTING STONES

You can set stone with just about any piece of equipment that you used to move it. Be prepared to do some adjusting and fine-tuning — if you're working with any kind of sling, leave the straps on until you're satisfied — and as you work, keep your mind open to new possibilities and nuances for your design. We often find that our plans don't realize their full potential until we're actually putting the stones into place and working hands-on with the texture and formation of stone and soil.

Instituting Drainage

Drainage would seem to be a small part of a stonescaper's concerns. After all, stones are heavy, so it will take a lot of water movement to unbalance one. Two problems, however, are ice and erosion.

When considering a stone feature in the North, you must think about what ice will do to the stone. Frost heaves — wintertime phenomena that occur when groundwater freezes, swelling and buckling the land around it — can move or even topple a stone, destroying the balance created by your well-planned efforts. The best way to avoid frost heaves, other than moving south, is to implement a good drainage system that moves water away from the stone as quickly as possible. This way water won't sit around the stone waiting to be frozen, and the stone should stay put.

If you live in an area where the soil doesn't drain well, you'll have to take precautions against erosion. If water collects on the surface of the soil, it tends to wear away at the surface, threatening the stability of your set stones.

In most cases, all you'll need for adequate drainage is well-draining soil or gravel around each stone. Stone formations that are primarily upright, use narrow columnar stone, or are set in heavy clay soil, however, will benefit from added measures of drainage.

Filter Fabric

One simple drainage system employs crushed stones and filter fabric. Filter fabric is a woven material that works much like a coffee filter: Ground stays above and water passes below. Dig the hole where the stone will be placed at least 18 inches (46 cm) deep and fill it with at least 6 inches (15 cm) of compacted crushed stones. Place a layer of filter fabric on top of the crushed stones, and then set your stone on top of the filter fabric. Cover with a top layer of loam for planting. The crushed stones allow water from the surface to filter quickly to the bottom of the hole away from the base of the stone; if it freezes there, it won't cause surface-level frost heaves. The filter fabric keeps the loam from sifting into and contaminating the stones.

Piping

When soils are too heavy or the grade isn't pitched for water movement, you may need to add piping to route water away from your stonescape. As when using filter fabric, dig a hole at least 18 inches (46 cm) deep and fill it with at least 6 inches (15 cm) of compacted crushed stone. Then dig a downward-sloping trench from the hole toward a run-off site, such as a stream or a man-made site (see page 110), and line the trench with at least 2 inches (5 cm) of crushed stone. Lay a 4-inch PVC pipe, also called an "elephant" pipe, in the trench. We've found that run-off pipes must drop at a rate of at least ¼-inch (6 mm) per foot to move water quickly enough that it won't freeze and clog the pipe. Measure the pitch of the pipe and adjust as necessary.

Once the pipe is laid, you may want to test the drainage by pouring water into and around the spot where the stone will rest. If you're satisfied with the movement of water, fill the trench around the pipe with crushed stone to within 4 inches (10 cm) of ground level. Then compact the crushed stone, using a hand tamp so that you won't crush the pipe, until you are sure all the air pockets have been removed. Place a layer of filter fabric over the crushed stone, set the stone, and then dress the top with loam.

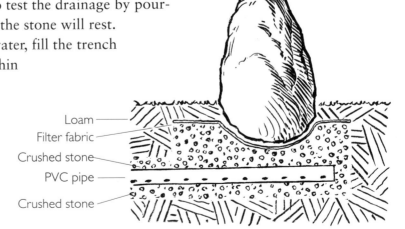

A cross-section of a drainage system using PVC pipe, crushed stone, and filter fabric

Loam
Filter fabric
Crushed stone
PVC pipe
Crushed stone

Building a Run-Off Site

If there will be a significant amount of water draining down a specific route from your site, a situation you may create if you institute drainage with piping, you may need to build a run-off site where that water can collect (rather than creating a swamp somewhere on the property). Dry wells and ponds are two of the most common run-off sites. Dry wells are used to gather and then distribute water via percolation. They can be made by digging a hole, lining the side walls with filter fabric, filling the hole with crushed stone, and topping off with more filter fabric and then 6 inches (15 cm) of loam. However, if the ground surrounding a dry well is saturated, the dry well effectively becomes a wet well and won't be any help with drainage. If your composition is sited in a relatively wet landscape or in an area that has more than its fair share of rainfall, a dry well becomes impractical. For this reason, we prefer using ponds as run-off sites.

From our perspective, a pond is a wonderful landscape feature in itself, and can even become the site of a complementary stone grouping. There are many different tips and techniques for building ponds of all sizes — if you're interested in building one, check out your local library or cooperative extension for further information.

Backfilling

If you're satisfied with the placement of the stones, you will be ready to *backfill,* or refill the hole around the stone. (If you're not satisfied with the placement, you'll need to adjust the stones — see page 113.) The material that you place in the hole around the stone is the *fill,* which is usually the same earth you dug out but can also be gravel (for drainage) or loam (for planting). You can use a backhoe, bulldozer, shovels — just about anything that moves earth — for backfilling. As you place the fill, tamp the earth down with the back of the shovel or a hand tamp.

Preventing Settling

Settling is a serious problem in areas of landfill reclaim and new construction. If the earth settles beneath a stone, it may cause the stone to shift, disrupting your stone composition. Compaction seems to be the best answer to this problem. If you live in an area of new construction, or one that has experienced settling, be sure to compact the material you put down as you backfill. The fill should be gravel that drains well but has sharp *fines,* or crushed or powdered stone, in it. What you don't want are round stones (compacting these is like compacting marbles) or a completely heavy silt soil such as clay.

A plate compactor

For smaller areas that don't have much more than 18 inches (46 cm) of backfill, you can use a plate compactor to compact the material going down. This is a machine about the size of a 10-horse rear-tine rototiller that has a large square vibrating plate. Put material down in layers no greater than 6 inches (15 cm) between compactions.

ADJUSTING THE PLACEMENT

Getting the stones in the ground is the largest part of your work, but once set, the stones may still need to be adjusted. You may want the angle of a stone to lean just a few more degrees, or may have trouble getting a vertical stone to stand up as straight as you want it to. Once you're satisfied with these finishing touches, you can plant any grasses, flowers, shrubs, or trees that you've chosen to complement your stonescape.

Roller Compactor

If you are excavating a large area, you may want to hire a contractor who has a roller compactor. Many excavation and paving companies have roller compactors and operators for hire. When you're working with a large area, they are well worth the money. They can compact larger areas in a shorter time with better results than can plate compactors.

Measuring Lines and Planes

Sometimes stone placements will require more than just an "eyeball" setting, and you'll need to measure the lines and angles of the stones to be sure that they are set "just so." For example, you may need to have just the right angle on a set of stones to build a greater sense of dynamic tension. Professionally, we work with a variety of site conditions that have every conceivable nuance that could be imagined, courtesy of many talented architects and designers. You may find that your own composition can be enhanced with just a slight adjustment of the set stones to perfect the lines and angles that intimate the subtleties of context, motivation, depth, and relationship. First, though, you'll need to be able to correctly measure those lines and angles.

Four-Foot Levels

The 4-foot (1.2 m) level is a tool no builder or mason can do without. This ingenious device, used to establish a level plane, is really nothing more than a rectangular bar with a tube of liquid, an air bubble in the liquid, and lines that tell you when the bubble is centered. You place the level on a surface and sight where the bubble is. If you want a surface to be perfectly horizontal, the bubble should be centered. When you're building steps, the level is invaluable in keeping them even and level. When you're placing stones, it is excellent for helping you maintain the desired angle of the top surface, and to get a fix on the vertical line of each stone.

A four-foot level

Transits, theodolites, and builder's levels are very accurate instruments used for measuring horizontal and vertical lines. You'll often see highway surveyors using them in areas slated for new-road construction. These precision tools are expensive, but can be rented in many communities. You will want someone with experience to help you learn how to use them. When you're doing a topographical survey of a property, these tools are a must. This type of survey is often necessary when you are dealing with features requiring elevation changes, such as hills or waterfalls. Mount these tools on a tripod with legs that you can adjust to the terrain to make the instrument level.

A pop-level

Pop-Levels

Pop-levels are well known in the masonry and landscaping fields, but not to the general public. They're small, cylinder-shaped tools about an inch (2.5 cm) across and 4 to 6 inches (10 to 15 cm) long — they look like small telescopes. Like line levels, pop-levels are used to establish level planes, such as between two stones or groupings of stones, but pop-levels can measure over greater distances than can line levels. To use this tool, you must first adjust it to your eye-level height. Then look through the telescope-tube; you'll see a hairline, a water bubble, and two lines for leveling. Adjust the telescope-tube so that the hairline is tangent to the top of your subject and the bubble is centered between the two lines, and you will have established a level plane between the tube and the far stone. Pop-levels range in cost and are fairly accurate. The transit (see box above) is more precise but also more expensive, and you'll need training to learn how to use it.

Line Level

A line level is like a miniature 4-foot (1.2 m) level that can be strung from a length of string or wire to measure the plane between two points. This tool should be in every mason's tool kit. It is readily available in hardware stores and is inexpensive. It is good for establishing a level plane over distances longer than your 4-foot level can measure. However, there are limitations to its accuracy. Imagine stretching a string over 30 feet (9 m), using stakes as anchors to keep the string from sagging. It is very near impossible. For this reason, if you are using a line level, keep the distances you are leveling no more than 8 to 10 feet (2.4 to 3.1 m). For anchors, use stable uprights such as grade stakes or trees.

When using a line level, make sure the string is taut.

Adjusting Set Stones

We've found that it's relatively impossible to foresee all the possible nuances of a stone and grouping until each stone is set in the ground, so we tend to make adjustments frequently. For this reason, if we've used webbing or straps to transport a stone, we never remove them until we've viewed the stone from all sides, and we never backfill unless we're positive that we're finished with our adjustments. If you do think you are finished with a grouping and backfill around a stone, only to discover afterward that you need to adjust it, you'll need to dig it back out. If this is the situation, a tractor with a pair of forks can be extremely helpful for large stones, while for smaller stones, a pry bar may be all you need. You can then spin, shift, or reset each stone until the placement is to your satisfaction.

Pry Bars

Pry bars are an absolute necessity when working with stones. These iron or steel bars are usually between 4 and 6 feet (1.2 and 1.8 m) long; they have a sharpened tip for stuffing into cracks and crannies on one end, and a flat or rounded end for pounding and grabbing on the other. Pry bars have incredible tensile strength, which means that when they're placed under great stress (such as the stress of trying to pry a boulder up out of the ground), they stay rigid and will not snap. It's important not to use a pry bar that's too small for the job — length and strength really do matter!

Pry bars are especially useful for shifting and adjusting stones. If you set a log or small stone on the ground to use as a fulcrum, you can use a pry bar as a lever to pry up the edge of a stone, either to shift it or to place a shim stone (see page 114) under it. Using two bars in tandem is an exceptionally successful and easy way to "walk" a rock. Here, two people get on either side of the stone, in turn placing their bars under it at an angle. The person on the right (relative to the direction you wish the stone to go) rotates the bar in a clockwise fashion, and the person on the left rotates counterclockwise. Repeat this process until the stone is in place.

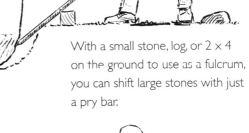

With a small stone, log, or 2 x 4 on the ground to use as a fulcrum, you can shift large stones with just a pry bar.

To "walk" a stone, take turns leveraging it forward from either side.

Shim stones can hold a stone in place until you can backfill around it.

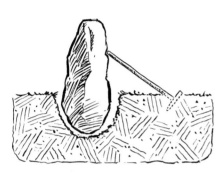

Bracing can also hold a stone in place until you are ready to backfill. As with a permanent base, you may want to bolt the brace to a wide, solid bottom to keep the brace from sinking into the ground.

Shim Stones

If a stone isn't sitting quite right, you will need to shim it. *Shimming* is the practice of using small to medium-size stones, called shim stones, as wedges to prop or shore up the misangled stone from below. You can often find stones usable for shimming among the broken pieces that will inevitably accompany the delivery of bulk stone.

Shim stones can help you achieve the appropriate angle or appearance, or they can hold a stone in place until it has been appropriately backfilled. When you place the wedges, be careful that they are secure and have not made the subject of your shimming tipsy or unstable.

Bracing

Sometimes if you're placing a stone with a high center of gravity or need an unusually steep angle, you may need bracing. The best material to use is another stone, but if that doesn't complement the dynamics of your composition, you can also try steel and pressure-treated wood braces, which are available at most lumberyards. If you know early on in your design that you're going to need bracing, try to incorporate the braces into your design. You'll want to either hide the material you're using or make it look like part of the composition.

When setting a brace, remember that it's friction and gravity that keep the brace in place. The surface area of contact between the brace and the stone will determine how stable the brace is. You may also consider bolting or otherwise fixing the brace to a wide, solid bottom to keep the brace from sinking into the ground. You can bury this base in an inch or two of topsoil to hide it.

SETTING STONES IN WATER

Stones and water are like salt and pepper, Abbot and Costello, yin and yang — you just don't see one without the other. If you have a pond, you should seriously consider adding some stones. There are many positive aspects to the combination — not least of which is simply giving you a place to sit and dangle your feet in the water on a hot summer evening. The question is how to get the stones into the water. Transporting stones over land is one thing, but moving stones across water may take some imagination.

Transporting in Large Spaces

If your water site is easily accessible and of reasonable size, the equipment you'll need to transport and set stones is pretty straightforward.

Cranes

There's nothing like a big old crane to do the stone lifting and placing in and around water. Not only is it good for moving stones of all sizes over land, but there's also nothing quite like it for setting stones out in the water. You will need a boat for this process, unless the water is of wading depth. As designers, we often need to be right in the water where the stones are to be placed. When the crane operator picks up a stone, you may have to adjust several times to get the sling under it for the best eventual presentation into the water. We also recommend that before releasing the stone, place it, still suspended, where you have designated it to go and look at it from all vantage points, taking the time to spin and adjust it as needed. This may frustrate your crane operator, but if you are forthright with your description of your expectations, he or she will be helpful and your end result will be worth the extra time.

Barges

If you are working in a body of water too big for a crane to reach the placement areas, you may need to contract with a barge or, even better, a barge with a crane. You may need a crane or a trackhoe to load the barge. Take the extra time required to put each stone on the barge just right so that when you offload into the water, the stone is placed for its best final presentation. If the barge is large enough, you may have the luxury of using a backhoe to offload the stone. If not, rig up a winch on the barge — some barges even have cranes with cable and hydraulics already aboard. Remember, you usually only get one shot when placing stones in water, particularly when working off a barge.

Getting Creative

If your water site is small, hard to get to, and inaccessible to cranes or barges, or if you are working with medium to small boulders that don't require the strength of a crane but still need to be floated out into the water, it's time for you to get really creative!

Rafts

If you have a small pond that is not accessible to a crane or barge, making a raft may be your best solution. The usual laws of physics and carpentry apply here, so don't be too hasty in the construction of your raft. Using Styrofoam or air-filled barrels can be helpful.

Pump

Pumping a pond down is an excellent way to make stone placement in the water easier. In some cases, you can wall off the particular section of the pond where you'll be building and pump down just that section. However, depending on the size and the location of the body of water, pumping down is not always practical. If there isn't a convenient place for you to pump the water to, don't do it. If you do pump your pond down, you can rent a sump pump for this purpose. They come in several different sizes. For the big jobs, though, you should call the professionals.

Long strips of flotation material, such as Styrofoam, can be used to make a sturdy, stable base for a raft used for moving stones.

Inner Tubes

A novel idea for moving stones in water is to make a floatable sling out of truck inner tubes. Such a sling should be very maneuverable for spinning the stones into place. You will probably get wet using this method, but pick a hot day and have some fun. Just watch your toes.

Setting and Maneuvering

We always keep snorkels, masks, and watertight flashlights handy for working with water. Even in shallow water they help with visibility, and for deeper water they're a must. Two quick cautions: One, don't kick up too much mud when you're in the water, or you'll never be able to see what you're doing; and two, keep your feet and fins clear when stone is being dropped into place.

Slides can make a simple task of maneuvering stones into place in a water setting.

Slides

Slides are a simple tool to use to place a larger stone in or along the edge of a pond. They can be constructed of metal, but wood will work for a job of limited duration. Slides can also make getting smaller stones from dry land out a few feet into the pond a much quicker process than shoveling them out would be.

Set the slide on a fulcrum, push the stone onto the land-based end, and then push the stone up, until the slide tips toward the water. Friction will usually keep the stone from immediately sliding off into the water, but watch out. Make sure the end of the stone that you want showing is pointed away from the water, and that the immersed end of the slide is settled at the spot you want the stone to be.

Gently push the stone down the rest of the slide — it will become easier to maneuver once it hits the water, but harder to see exactly where it's headed. Once the stone is set in the ground, you can use the slide to prop it in place until you can backfill around it. When it's stable, remove the slide.

Pry Bars

Be prepared to place stones in water and then find out you need to move or spin them. It happens. When it does, have your pry bars handy. The same principles that apply on land apply in the water. Leverage is your secret weapon, and in the water you will need it.

Three Stone Placement Examples

7

One of the best ways to understand the process of stone placement is to witness it. This chapter will describe the entire process — both the thought process and the physical — of putting a stone composition in the ground. The project described here was installed at one of our office entryways, and consisted of three separate yet connected groupings. The entire composition took about six hours to set in the ground. Two of them were done by hand using shovels and pry bars. The third grouping included large stones (1½ to 2 tons [1,362 to 1,816 kg]) that called for motorized equipment in combination with shovels and pry bars.

ORDERING THE STONE

A trip to the stone supplier was our first step — in this case, a three hour drive from Lexington, South Carolina, to Asheville, North Carolina. At the center, a variety of stones were scattered on the ground, pallets of flat stones were ready for shipping, and people were busy preparing more stones to be shipped. One particular type of stone, from an area known as Fines Creek in North Carolina, caught our eye. It was angular and had mosses and lichens on its surface. We ordered 16 tons (14,515 kg) of this type of stone, to be delivered within a few days, simply on the basis of this one stone. We didn't pick out individual stones, relying instead on the luck of the draw.

The angles of repose of the piled stones formed implied planes and lines of force that made the entire mass look like one eroded grouping.

DELIVERY

The stones arrived in a large multi-axle dump truck and were unceremoniously dumped in an area of the yard that would be central to the location of each of the arrangements. A curious phenomenon occurred once the stones were actually on the ground. They came in a mixture of sizes, from 100 pounds (45 kg) up to 2 tons (1,816 kg), and the way they all lay out relative to each other was actually a stone formation in its own right. When aggregate material is dumped in place, its ultimate shape is determined by something called its *angle of repose*: the angle at which the material is stable. If you try to make that angle too steep, it will collapse on itself and reassume the appropriate angle of repose. The same thing occurred with this delivery of stones — except, of course, on a larger scale — and the pile took on characteristics of a natural stone formation.

ANALYZING THE STONE

In order to make our placement choices, we needed to spread the stones out over the area. We used a bobcat loader with pallet forks to pick up individual stones and distribute them evenly around the site. This is important because it gave us enough room to completely walk around each stone. We turned each of the rocks until it showed its most desirable face — usually the face with the lichen and mosses showing, although this was not always true, and we had to examine each stone separately. Some stones, for instance, had certain cleavages or embedded elements that we felt took precedence over the plant growth on their surface. In addition, we took a mental inventory of the best orientation for each stone. Some stones have an upright character, others tend to be chunky horizontal masses, and still others are low, flat, foreground elements. We also noted which stones were versatile enough to be used in a variety of ways. Then it was time to take a fresh look at the site where the stones were going to be placed.

SITE REVIEW

The site is the front entry and exit of a home and home office. It is a bit unusual in that the grade rises as you move away from the foundation. Most structures have grades that slope away from the foundation, to facilitate drainage. In this case, water drained around the side of the house. This downgrade toward the building was, for us, a key factor in determining the underlying motivation of the stone groupings that we'd place here, because we decided to later build a stream and waterfall that mimicked the natural flow of the land down toward the house.

A secondary factor influencing the development of our design was the site's walkway. Walkways are powerful spaces commanding attention. Because of this, the walkway outside the office affected the rhythm of the stones and their spacing as well as the subsequent dynamic grouping of the disparate elements into a unified whole. In many respects, the placement of the stones would help define the walkway, and the walkway would help define and recognize the underlying context of the stones themselves.

Once you have a basic understanding of the site, you need to take a look at where the stones would have the most impact. In this site there were three primary locations that would benefit from the addition of some rocks:

- The entry zone — from the driveway to the entry walk
- The transition zone — along the walkway
- The office zone's three points of view — entry, exit, and office window

Pathways and Stone Groupings

A formal walkway is a strong element and exudes a great deal of flowing energy. Because of this, you must give considerable weight to the effect of a walkway on a space as a whole. Start by looking at nature: If you note where naturally occurring walkways and paths tend to be relative to stones and rocks, you'll begin to see the most logical way to place stones relative to the path you are working with. In a natural environment, a pathway follows the course of least resistance. Adjacent to stones, cliffs, and other rocky features, it tends to follow cleavage or fracture lines in the larger geological formation. These cleavage points tend to fill with eroded material, leaves, and other organic matter. As they fill, the original fracture becomes obscured; it is only hinted at by the protruding stones that surround it. Understanding this is critical to creating a meaningful stone grouping adjacent to a more contrived path. All stone placements should imply an overall underlying structure that makes sense on a subconscious or subliminal level.

This is the entry before construction began. The beginning of the path, next to the stone wall, marks the entry zone, where the first grouping will be sited. As you proceed down the path, you pass through the transition zone, where the second grouping will be sited. As you approach the office door at the end of the path, you walk by the site of the third grouping.

Entry Zone

The pathway begins at the driveway; as you face the house, the path rises slightly to the right, then turns to the left. It ascends through and alongside some low stone walls. Metaphorically, the walkway is a waterfall. As we looked at this space, some of our key considerations were the primary perspective (people entering the space), secondary perspective (people exiting the space), and tertiary perspective (people driving up to the entry area). Another key component was the existing stone walls. In particular, there was a single stone in the wall that set a tone and eventually became the beginning of a unified pattern.

Transition Zone

There is a strong linear flow to the walkway as it passes between the exterior of the garage and a low, dry-stacked stone wall. Metaphorically, in this case, the walkway is a fast-flowing river. Some of our key considerations were the primary and secondary perspectives (entry and exit), the existing wall, and the turn in the walk heading toward the door of the house and its office.

Viewed Grouping

When the grouping is finished, it will not be entirely visible from the walkway as you enter into the space. It will only be visible as a whole from inside the office looking out the window, on the porch immediately outside the office window, or as you exit the building and walk down the pathway.

THE INSTALLATIONS

Although the three groupings of stone are connected, they each form their own composition. Following is a description of the stone-by-stone placement.

▶ SITE ONE: Earth Dragon Diving

Upon considering the fluid energy of the walkway, the image that immediately came to mind was a dragon diving and swimming through the earth as though it were as fluid as water. This is an inverse form of Hag's Reckoning (see page 153).

Plan of site 1 grouping

Stone One

In choosing the first stone, we gave careful consideration to the scale of the space. Since the first stone would drive all of our subsequent choices, it was important that it not be too large. If the stone was 4 or 5 feet (1.2 to 1.5 m) tall, and we wanted to maintain pleasing ratios, it is likely that our

STONE 1. We dug an uneven hole for stone 1 so that its lichen-covered surface would face the viewer approaching the path.

STONE 1. Here is stone 1 set in place. You can see what will become stone 2, a preexisting element of the wall, to the left.

smallest stones would have been too big for the rather intimate area of a front entry. Ultimately we chose a stone that would rise 2½ to 3 feet (76 to 91 cm) out of the ground. The strong downward-sloping angle in toward the walkway and stairs that we used was based on the energy and weight of the walk surface. A natural path usually occurs in the filled fissures of a larger stone mass, so it was logical for us to duplicate that. This essentially established the primary line of force for this grouping. We chose the face of the stone because of the nice arrangement of lichens on its surface; we angled this face to show to best advantage from the primary point of view, the entry area. We also considered the perspective of an exiting viewer, but gave this secondary importance.

STONE 2. With a little adjustment, a stone already in the wall becomes stone 2 of the grouping. It mimics and reinforces the angles and planes of stone 1.

Stone Two

The second stone was already in place — it was part of the existing wall at the top of the stairs. It needed adjustment, however, to become more in tune with the lines of force established by the first stone. In order to create a relationship between the two stones, we turned and twisted stone 2 until its inside angle roughly matched and reinforced the corresponding angle in stone 1. In this way the outside edge of the second stone arced upward with a minor implied plane that subtly connected it to the first stone.

Stone Three

We placed the third stone in front of the lower wall to provide some foreground interest and create a greater sense of depth within the entry space. The height of this stone was important — it had to be low enough so viewers could look over it to see the wall beyond. Since stone 3 was also directly adjacent to the walk, it needed a certain amount of character as well. We ended up choosing a chunky stone that had some interesting horizontal planes at different heights. These planes reinforced the horizontal plane of the wall behind it. Another nice thing about this stone was that it had a flat bottom and only needed to be buried to a depth of about 2 inches (5 cm). Its final placement also had to somehow tie in to the lines of force expressed in the first two stones. We found that the left side of stone 3, the side closest to the walk, needed very little adjustment to mimic the angle of stone 2. Now, as you can see in the photograph below, stones 1, 2, and 3 each seem to lean in the same direction.

STONE 3. We set stone 3 in the ground below the wall. The angle of its left edge repeats the angles of stones 1 and 2, helping to tie it in to the grouping.

Stone Four

The fourth stone needed to establish and maintain a sense of middle ground to give more depth to the space. We chose a spot midway between the wall and the first stone. In a sense, stone 4 reflected stone 1. In nature, stones often fracture and separate due to water's freezing and thawing action. A stone that is thus cleaved from the surface will maintain all of the characteristics of its parent stone (similar to the slump block of a cliff). Stone 4 is 38 percent of the height of stone 1. This ratio tends to be pleasing to the eye, and it would also allow a better display of the first stone when we subsequently planted evergreens. Of course, we used the same line of force in this stone as in all the others.

Stone Five

The fifth stone needed to provide some background repetition in order to reinforce the depth that we had started with stones 3 and 4. The negative space created between the first stone and the fifth stone was very powerful, and would be important later when we placed the connecting texture of a planting within this space. We based the height of stone 5 on the viewer's perspective

STONES 4 AND 5. Stone 4 establishes a sense of midground and Stone 5, of background, helping the viewer see the depth of the composition. Together, they begin to establish a picture of the composition as a vein of stone jutting out of the ground along a common line. Stones 1, 3, 4, and 5 follow along that line.

entering the walkway. The stone had to be subordinate to the first stone — it could not visually rise above stone 1 even though it was farther up the slope. Ultimately, we placed stone 5 so that its top line would match a horizontal surface feature on the front of the first stone. We also angled stone 5 to reflect the lines of force established by the first four stones and add to the continuity of the mass grouping.

Stone Six

The sixth stone in the grouping was placed the farthest forward of any of the stones. In a manner of speaking, stone 6 frames and contains the pool of energy that creates a sense of place in that entry environment. It follows a logical height transition toward the more distant stones and is angled to lead the eye into the rest of the composition. We placed it roughly along the same vein as stones 1, 3, 4, and 5.

Stone Seven

The seventh stone was critical because there was too much negative space between stones 1 and 2. The eye tended to be drawn into this area; what the eye needed instead was to be diverted to the group as a whole. By placing a stone that was in the midrange of height between stones 1 and 2, we created a visual bridge. The top line of stone 7 also met with the implied plane established between stones 1 and 2, thus reinforcing that relationship. Of course, we adhered to the original lines of force.

Stone Eight

We placed the eighth stone at the left of the top of the entry area to better contain the space. It reinforces the idea that there was a cleavage in the stone mass below, and the walkway and entry stairs were logically placed within that fracture line. The dominant angle of stone 8 complemented the angles we established in the line of force of stones 1, 2, 3, 4, 5, and 7. Where these two lines of force meet below the earth becomes an imaginary fault line. This secondary line of force is complemented in the top lines of stones 3 and 6 when viewed from the opposite (secondary) perspective.

STONES 6 AND 7. Stone 6 helps contain the space in the immediate entry area, while stone 7 builds a visual bridge between stones 1 and 2, filling the negative space.

Stones 1 through 8 viewed from the secondary (exiting) perspective. Stone 8 falls in the lower right-hand shadows of the view. From this view, its top line mimics the angles of stones 3 and 6 set farther ahead below the stone wall.

STONE 9. This smaller stone is set just a step or two down the path from stone 8, helping to fill out the viewer's sense of the grouping as a unified composition.

Stone Nine

The final stone in this grouping is mostly incidental and serves to enhance the overall composition. Its greatest purpose is to create depth along the walkway. It also unifies site 1 and site 2 by picking up certain lines of sight. Finally, it helps frame the view down the walkway, even though it is relatively small in stature.

The Overall Composition

The total grouping is primarily made up of the first seven stones; the two final stones really don't come into play until you make the turn and climb the stairs. The composition will not be complete, however, until the Japanese maple is planted (note the position of the pry bar). The top line of the first and most dominant stone will be repeated in the angle of the branch that will serve to contain the entry space from overhead. The branch on the tree will also be trained to mimic and repeat the implied plane established between stones 1, 2, and 7.

SITE 1. As you approach the path, your attention is drawn to the first seven stones of the composition. In a few years, these stones will be strongly supported by the Japanese maple that will be planted at the spot marked by the pry bar.

▶ SITE TWO: Sunken Valley

The sunken valley is a cleavage in the earth that forms a foundation for the pathway that runs over it.

Stone One

The first stone in this grouping is not the dominant stone; rather, it helps establish a tone or sequence for the subsequent stones. It lies within the plane of the walkway and thus helps make the stone grouping more intimate to visitors who enter the space. We also wanted to repeat the theme established by the first stone grouping — that this walkway sits upon a cleavage in the earth. So the first line of force in this arrangement leads from the center of and below the walkway off to the right (from the primary point of view — perspective of someone entering the space from the driveway).

Plan of site 2 grouping

STONE 1. Stone 1 is a long, horizontal stone that sits below the stone wall, directing a line of force into the center of the walkway.

We placed stone 2 in front of stone 1 (from the primary p.o.v.) as a more dominant purveyor of the line of force that meets the flowing energy of the walkway.

Stone Two

The second stone is more dominant but defines the outer limits of the placement. It juts forth, with its inside edge following the same line of force we established with stone 1. We also placed stone 2 along the same vein of stone established by stone 1. In other words, we repeated the angle of the first stone relative to the direction of travel along the walkway. All subsequent stones will repeat along this same vein.

Stone Three

The third stone is also a dominant stone, but subordinate to stone 2 in terms of height. It establishes a second line of force complementary to the first. When all is said and done, the two lines of force will appear to join below the surface of the walkway.

Stone Four

The fourth stone is a transition stone that helps lead the eye in toward the walkway's surface. The overall face of stone 4 mimics the plane established by the third stone, but also contains another plane that lies roughly perpendicular to the plane establishing the second line of force. This second plane is found in both stones 3 and 4, and its repetition is critical to reinforcing the relationship between these two stones and the group as a whole.

Stone Five

The fifth and final stone in the grouping is a transition stone that leads the eye into the space around the corner relative to the walk to the front door. It helps soften the harsh angle of stone 3 and creates a dynamic tension between these two stones: It appears that they were one stone at some point in the past but have since separated. It is important to note here that all five of the stones essentially lie along the same vein within the ground. This helps establish them as a unified grouping.

The Overall Composition

In many respects, this composition of five stones helps frame the entire walk as you enter the space. The sense of cleavage creates a nested feeling and sense of security. If additional stones were placed, they would be used as a foreground element to add more depth to the composition. But successful stone groupings do not all need to be nine stones. Sometimes you just need to know when to stop.

STONES 3, 4, AND 5. These three stones are situated across the walkway from stones 1 and 2. Not only do they create a second line of force that meets the first line of force (created by stones 1 and 2) in the center of the walkway but, as a group of three, they show an internal dynamic tension.

SITE 2. The finished grouping at site 2 reinforces the idea that the path forges through a cleavage in what was once a larger mass.

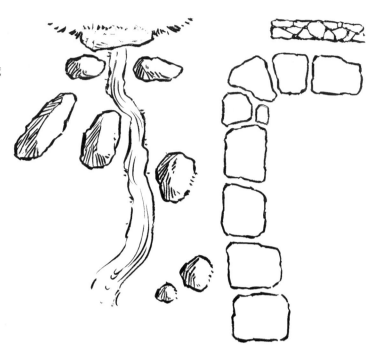

Plan of site 3 grouping, showing eventual placement of hillside and stream

▶ SITE THREE: Gates of Sumeru

The Islands of the Immortals is a metaphoric element used in stone arrangements in early Japanese gardens that symbolized longevity and immortality. In some arrangements, generally recumbent stones would circle one focal stone and as a group would be known as the Islands of the Immortals. The central island was known to be the mountain called Mount Sumeru.

This stone arrangement's primary purpose was to create a focal point from the point of view inside the home office that reflected the character and nature of the business conducted there — landscape design and stone placement. This became the primary point of view. Although this composition is currently visible at the end of the straight walkway, it will not remain so once it is finished.

The final composition will not be a freestanding stone grouping but rather a 3½- to 4-foot (1 to 1.2 m) waterfall. There will be soil and a stream coming from above and behind it. Hillside and peninsula will descend from right to left as you face the arrangement and will contain stones that mimic the current composition. The important thing to note here is that although the final grouping can stand on its own, it is not the end of the process. The freestanding grouping described here will eventually blend with a larger whole that will be influenced by the angles and forms of the initial freestanding stones. In essence, this third grouping is the skeleton that guides the creation of the final body.

Stone One

We wanted the first stone to reflect the character and nature of the water-fall that was our end strategy. Therefore, stone 1 needed to be vertical in nature because the topography did not lend itself to a broad waterfall. A vertical waterfall is also far more effective as a focal point. We put a great deal of thought and consideration into the selection of this stone. Still, at first glance you might think we chose wrong: All of stone 1's nice mosses and lichens seem best suited to a horizontal mass. But stone 2 had an interesting surface — two planes cut into its sides — and those features could match up very well with another stone we had in mind for the final arrangement. That took precedence over the mosses and lichens. Also, stone 1 was tapered with one straight side, and had an interesting top feature that we could eventually use in the grouping.

STONE 1. This stone weighed in at about 1½ tons (681 kg), so we placed it using a bobcat with forks. (We both have considerable experience using one, or else we would have chosen a simpler tool.) We laid the stone down perpendicular to the hole, then brought the bobcat from behind to lift it slowly into place. Once vertical, we used shim stones and a pry bar to stabilize the stone.

STONE 2. We needed the bobcat loader again for pushing stone 2 into the hole we'd dug for it.

Stone Two

The second stone we chose could, if set properly, aptly mirror the lines and planes of stone 1. This stone was also large enough that we needed to use a bobcat loader to move it. When we excavated the hole, we gave careful consideration to digging its bottom such that stone 2's top line would fall naturally into place without a great deal of final adjusting.

Setting the second stone so that its angles and lines were appropriate was critical. On our first try we managed to successfully align the two embedded planes in stone 1 with the top line and surface features of stone 2. We then needed only to fine-tune and backfill.

Notice how the angles and planes of stones 1 and 2 mirror each other, creating strong lines of force and a great sense of connection.

Stone Three

The third stone had to serve several purposes. First, it needed to be a backdrop for the waterfall, and would ultimately serve as the guide for its final height. Second, the stone needed to serve as a visual transition between stone 1 and stone 2 in the group's descent from left to right. Third, it had to provide a logical motivation for the descent of the slope that would be behind it. We chose a stone about 2 tons (1,816 kg) in weight. It was very simple to place; the critical factors were its ultimate height and making sure its top line would accommodate a waterfall. Only minor adjustments were necessary to assure a level top line, and since the chosen stone was so uniform and flat bottomed, our excavation was straightforward as well.

STONE 3. As seen here, stone 3 becomes a backdrop for stones 1 and 2 and serves as a transition in their descent.

Stone Four

The fourth stone in the group would be seen from at least three perspectives, including that of anyone walking up the pathway to the home office entrance. Thus we wanted to somehow reflect the angles of the stones in the first two compositions in stone 4 as well. This stone also needed to be of a unique character. We chose a stone that had a great deal of quartz in it, along with a top line of considerable interest. Its primary role from the main perspective was to create some middle ground; also, the stream that would someday flow from the waterfall would be diverted toward the walkway by this stone.

STONE 4. The seating of stone 4 was fairly straightforward, but it took us considerable effort to adjust its height and top line to accommodate the three perspectives. This stone weighed 1 ton (908 kg), and we spent a great deal of time working on it with a pry bar.

Stone Five

The role of stone 5 was to contain the composition and lead the eye naturally into the group, funnelling attention from the midground to the backdrop. Since it would also be visible from the entrance along the walkway, we had to consider exactly how we would impart the angles and theme established by our first two groupings into stone 5.

Since stone 5 weighed close to 2 tons (1,816 kg), we didn't want to have to move it around a lot once it was placed. The problem with the stone that we chose was also its strong suit: a very interesting angle. In order to place the stone properly, we had to set one side of its bottom very deep, and the other end of its bottom only a couple of inches (cm) down.

Stone Six

The sixth stone in the group was more a foreground stone. It was a response to the presence of stone 4 in that, if the stream was diverted toward the walkway, something had to receive it and give the stream a reason to straighten out.

We chose a low horizontal stone with interesting side faces so that we could extend the level of the walkway out into the stream. This would allow both visual and physical access to the water.

The placement was straightforward, although we had to remember that this would be the shore of a stream. As such,

STONE 5. We spent a great deal of time measuring and digging to make sure stone 5's desired top line would fall naturally into place when we slid it into its hole.

STONE 5. After carefully preparing the hole, we gently set stone 5 with the bobcat loader.

part of the stone would be embedded in the banking, but a large part of it would be exposed to the stream. When the entire piece is completed, it will be critical to have a few other stones adjacent to this platform stone. They will not only guide the visitor to the water's edge but also visually frame the view of the stream from at least two perspectives.

Stone Seven

The seventh stone in the grouping serves as a foreground and framing element from the secondary perspective (as you leave the home office). It also greets the visitor from the tertiary perspective. Thus, the stone had to be fairly vertical in nature, but at the same time had to lend a commonality to all the stones set before it. Since stone 7 is adjacent to the walkway, it was also important that it have some interest to its face.

STONES 5 AND 6. We ran into a bit of luck because although we paid considerable attention to stone 5's ascending top line, we paid very little to the adjacent angle. It turned out that this other angle was perfectly horizontal. The stone will thus serve as a wonderful bench once the whole composition is put together. We then began making ready for stone 6, which will become part of the stream's banking.

STONE 7. In order to get the height right, we had to put nearly half of stone 7 in the ground

As you approach the path to the office, you see the first seven stones of site 1, most of site 2, and a glimpse of site 3.

As you travel down the walkway, you see stones 8 and 9 of site 1 and realize that the grouping is larger than you thought. As you see sites 2 and 3 in the distance, you may begin to understand what the stones are telling you — that this path routes through the natural cleavage of an eroding larger mass.

The planes of site 2 direct you around the corner of the path head-on into site 3, just outside the door to the office. The energy of travel flowing down the path is caught and directed by the stones of this grouping (and eventually, by the waterfall and stream) straight toward the entryway.

INTEGRATING ALL THREE COMPOSITIONS

Once we had placed the majority of the stones, it was important to follow up on the integration of all our elements. Adjustments needed to be made that would accomplish our ultimate goal: a composition in which everything worked together and spoke to the internal relationships all the stones shared.

After we looked down the walkway from the entrance, we adjusted stone 8 in the first composition slightly, to better match the angle of stone 4 in the second composition. Stone 9 (first grouping) was adjusted as well, to better configure to the angle of stone 1 (second grouping) and stone 5 (third grouping). Stone 2 (second grouping) also needed some adjustment, to better coordinate the angle of its top line to that of stone 5 (third grouping).

CONCLUSION

A good deal of critical thinking goes into creating a successful stone composition, but the critical path involves the following:

1. Understand the space you are working in.
2. Determine a line of force.
3. Have a general direction in mind.
4. The first stone you choose will be a driving force in the stone choices that follow, as well as in the subsequent placement of all the stones to follow.
5. Don't be afraid to make adjustments after the fact in order to fine-tune all the aspects that will unify the composition.

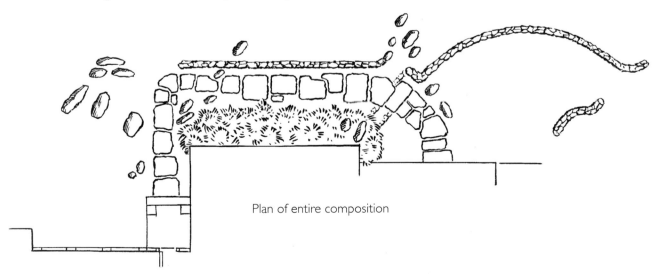

Plan of entire composition

Stone Grouping Design Ideas

8

Design ideas are often derived from the space-defining qualities of the site where you'll place your grouping. There are essentially four environments that may govern your design:

- A flat plane
- A connective mass within a flat plane
- A sloping plane
- Transition of sloping plane with a flat plane

Every site you examine is likely to be a variation of one of these environments. In order to understand these spaces better, think of them in more familiar terms. A flat plane could be equated to a pond, a lawn, a patio, a planting bed, or a swimming pool surface. A connective mass within a flat plane is an island form — think of a real island in water or a planting island in a lawn. A sloping plane can be thought of simply as a hillside; the relative steepness of that slope may vary. Finally, the sloping plane joining the flat plane can be likened to the shoreline of a pond or the ocean. It could also be a spot where a hill joins a flat lawn or planted bed.

In each case, the evolution of your design will be influenced by the characteristics of that space. The motivation of the form that you create has its roots in a study known as geomorphology, which looks at how the earth is shaped and formed through processes such as weathering and erosion. In the case of stone groupings, these processes wear away the parent mass, leaving the sturdier remnants that reveal its internal

structure. When you see a natural stone formation, you are seeing the result of eons of
active degradation and entropy. In attempting
to re-create this natural form, you are also
trying to imbue the composition with some of
the same qualities inherent in the original.
Primary among those attributes is a feeling of
great age.

This chapter is organized by these four
basic environments. We give five examples of
stone arrangements inspired by each of these
environments as well as a brief explanation
addressing the motivation of each design. A
plan will show the grouping's layout, and a
perspective will sketch each composition from
its primary point of view. Each diagram
points out the lines of force that unify the
arrangement, and the stones are numbered so
that you can see the evolution of the grouping
from three through nine stones.

The stones depicted in these design ideas
are not intended to serve as models for the
stones you'll use in your groupings, should
you decide to work with one of these plans.
Remember, these are simply *ideas* for plans.
As you visualize the placement of stones in
your space, you will have to take into account
the limitations and amenities of the site and
the purpose of the completed grouping. The
stones illustrated in these perspectives and
plans will show you the dynamic arrangement
of each idea — the spacing, size, and location
of the stones. Your final design must be
guided by the stones you have on-hand to
work with.

Don't think that these ideas are the full
extent of what is possible — not by a long
shot. They should serve as models that you
can try in your own landscape, or as catalysts
that will launch you down your own road to
creative applications.

Flat plane

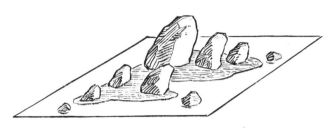

Connective mass

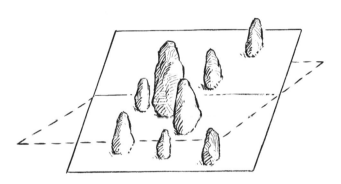

Sloping plane

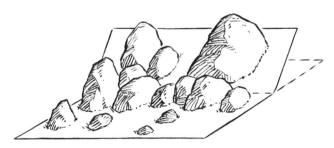

Transition of sloping
plane with flat plane

Although each of these designs is featured with nine stones, they can also be built with three, five, or seven stones. To help you visualize the evolution of each design, and any of its smaller variations, the stones are numbered. To see what a design looks like with only the first five stones, for example, cover stones 6, 7, 8, and 9 with your hands (some designs require more dexterity than others). The size of the stones you use will have to depend on the scale of the site.

▶ WORKING WITH A FLAT PLANE

Faded Monolith

Motivation: A tall mountain undergoing erosion.

Application: This would be good as a focal point, in a pond, in a planting bed, outside an entryway, or in a meditation garden.

Description: The mountain core and a few remnant elements are all that is left. The implied planes of the outer stones serve to connect the stones and allude to a past parent mass. The lines of force all lead into the central core. The motivation can be carried by a grouping of three stones. Stones 4 and 5 serve to expand the base, as do stones 6 and 7. Stones 8 and 9 are appropriate if there is enough space for greater breadth, and also serve to create a foreground from the primary point of view.

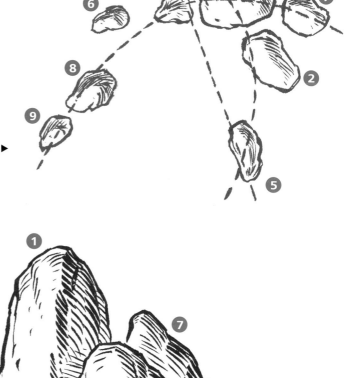

PLAN ▶

PERSPECTIVE ▼

Crying Mountain

Motivation: An eroding mountain range disappearing into the sea.

Application: This type of grouping (and variations on it) works well in medians or in long, narrow spaces.

Description: The core of this grouping is a horizontal mass that gives direction to the evolution of the rest of the arrangement. The lines of force and the implied planes are more rounded and less defined, intimating to the viewer that the individual stones were separate peaks at one time. Stones 1, 2, and 3 provide the basic structure, and stones 4 through 9 serve to reinforce the theme.

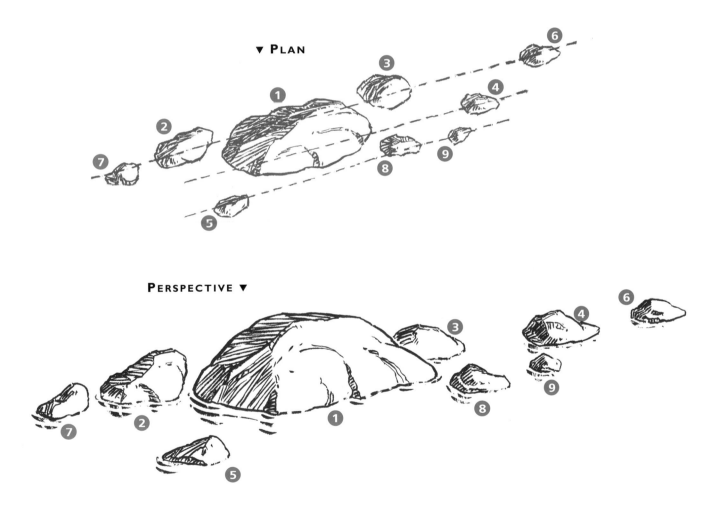

▼ **PLAN**

PERSPECTIVE ▼

Vulcan Necklace

Motivation: The submerged or covered caldera of an ancient volcano.

Application: This works well as a primary focal point or as a meditative device.

Description: The Vulcan Necklace was inspired by Molikini, a volcano off the island of Hawaii. Although the crater of Molikini is not really a caldera (it's actually a steam vent), it sure looks like something big went off in the middle of it. The external lines of force radiate outward and the internal lines of force upward from a central point below the grouping. Most groupings that are volcanic in motivation are very movement oriented. Although this grouping works with just the first three stones, using at least five will better communicate the intent. Stones 6 and 7 emphasize the shape, and stones 8 and 9 extend the leading edge of movement.

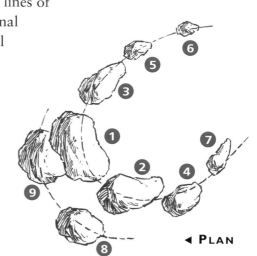

◄ PLAN

PERSPECTIVE ▼

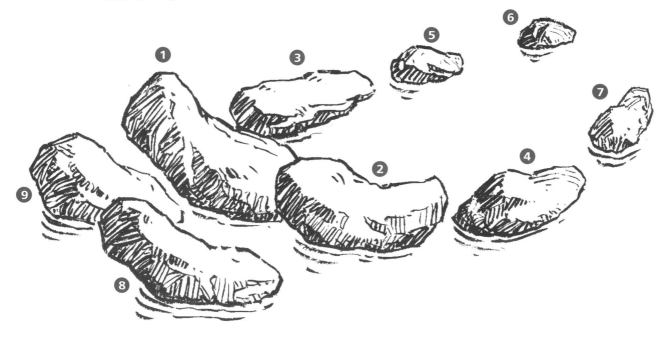

Pillars of Sumeru

Motivation: The basaltic columns that remain from an ancient upward-swelling intrusion.

Application: This is a striking arrangement that works well as a focal point. At the right scale, it could be placed in water so that only the tops of the stones are above water, lending an ethereal and mysterious quality to their submerged bases.

Description: The inspiration for our grouping's name arises from the Japanese myth of the Islands of the Immortals, whose central island is called Mount Sumeru. The internal lines of force are all vertical and run parallel to each other, emanating from the core of the earth. Stone 2 is at 62 percent of the height of stone 1, and stone 3 is at 62 percent of the height of stone 2. The remaining stones are more involved with unifying the composition, although stone 5 should be at 31 percent the height of stone 2. Stones 8 and 9 serve to emphasize the implied planes that hint at a parent-mass predecessor that once connected each of the now separate elements.

◄ **PLAN**

◄ **PERSPECTIVE**

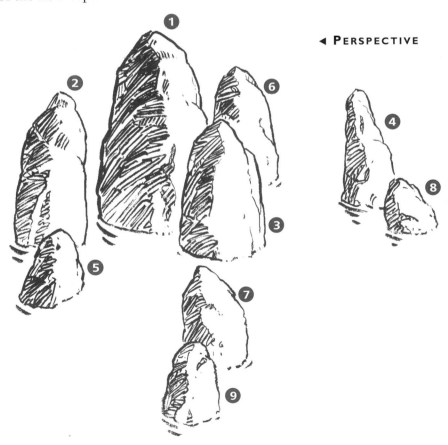

Notice how the differing use of implied planes in Swimming Dragons and Orca (facing page) create different impressions of movement. In Swimming Dragons, stone 1 and all of the stones to its left point to the right, implying planes between each of the stones in the three rows. All of the stones to the right of stone 1 point to the left, back toward stone 1, implying planes in the opposite direction. In the arc of the intersecting planes, you can almost see the undulating curve of the dragons' backs as they slip in and out of the water.

In Orca, all of the stones point in the same direction, with several implied planes connecting the stones to each other. In this case, you get a great sense of rising movement, as if there were some great force below pushing the stones up and forward.

Swimming Dragons

Motivation: Similar to Crying Mountain (an eroding mountain range; see page 141), but more intimate and at a much closer scale.

Application: This type of grouping (and variations on it) works well in medians or in long, narrow spaces.

Description: Swimming Dragons refers to the three basic underlying forms that move from left to right, and is simply a device for remembering and conveying the content of this group. Notice that there are three distinct lines of force all moving in the same direction. Stones 1, 2, and 3 establish the basic form of the middle dragon. Stones 4 and 5, as part of the second dragon, help define a space between the two. Stones 6 and 7 add the final dragon; because part of its body is obscured by the first, it appears that there may be more that is hidden. Stones 8 and 9 add emphasis to the direction of movement and flesh out the second dragon.

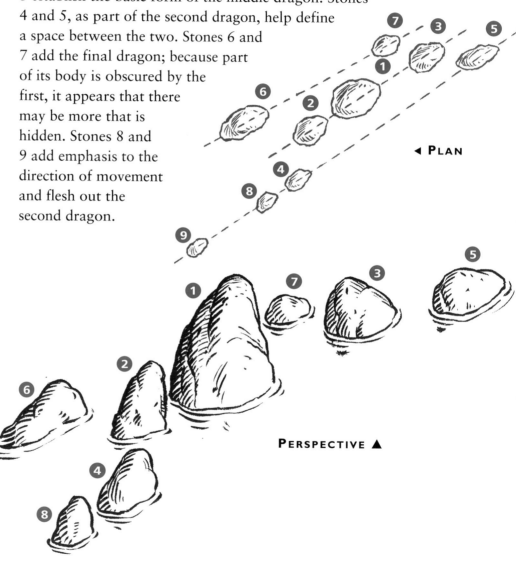

◄ **PLAN**

PERSPECTIVE ▲

▶ WORKING WITH A CONNECTIVE MASS

Orca

Motivation: The way that killer whales move through the water in a pack.

Application: This can work well in almost any well-framed environment but, because of its strong use of movement, is especially effective along walks.

Description: This formation uses strong, angular forms that point in a similar direction to create a strong sense of movement. The internal lines of force for this grouping emanate from below the ground and arc outward. Stones 1, 2, and 3 draw attention to the island and establish a theme immediately. Stones 4 and 5 finish off the island. Stones 6 and 7 suggest a larger connective mass that unifies the composition, while stones 8 and 9 reinforce that concept.

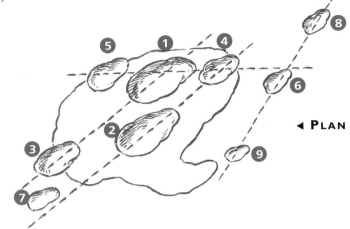

◀ **PLAN**

PERSPECTIVE ▼

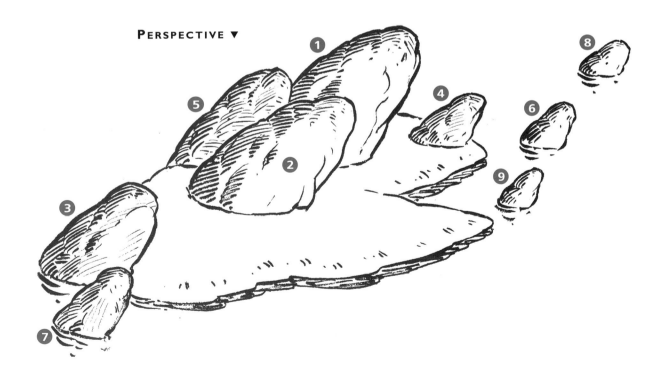

Stone Flower

Motivation: An internal form that radiates outward from somewhere deep within a parent mass.

Application: This makes a good planting bed arrangement surrounded by a ground cover of some type.

Description: Stone Flower's internal lines of force can be likened to remnants of an explosion from a long time ago and resemble the petals of a flower. By using two islands, you create a dramatic sense of dynamic tension between the two — the two islands appear to be in the act of separating, but the angles of the stones still unify them. Stones 1, 2, and 3 emphasize the lines of force and provide a good focal point. Stones 4 and 5 consolidate the main island and introduce the second island as a connected element. Stones 6 and 7 further emphasize the lines of force and the unity of the composition; stones 8 and 9 enlarge the relationship to spaces beyond the islands.

Garden Beds

In this illustration, Stone Flower is set in water, as it might be found in the shallows of a pond or small brook. However, Stone Flower also makes a dramatic garden feature — just build small, raised garden beds as the islands, set the stones, and then surround them with bright flowers and ground covers. The brighter the surrounding plantings are, the more explosive seems the power that created Stone Flower.

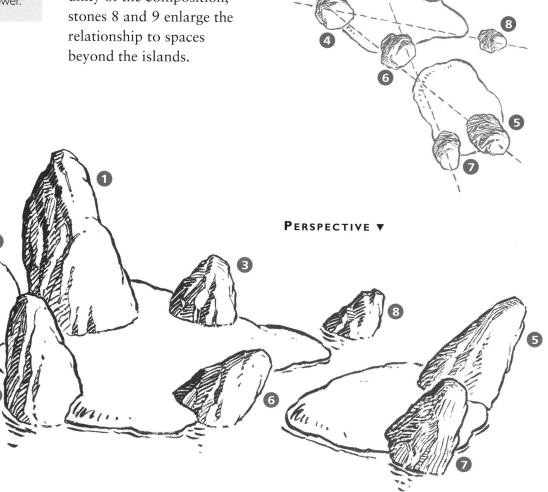

◄ **PLAN**

PERSPECTIVE ▼

Phoenix Rising

Motivation: A slump block separating from the main mass of a promontory.

Application: This type of arrangement lends itself best to a solitary perspective and use as a meditative device.

Description: Forces of erosion tend to cleave stone along fissure lines, and that's what's going on here. As the nature of the piece is very vertical, we were inspired to name it after the legend of the Phoenix that rises from its ashes. The external lines of force arc toward the central core of stone 1. Supporting stones 2 and 3 serve to consolidate and define the previous whole. Stones 4 and 5 provide emphasis and movement along those lines of force. Stones 6 and 7 help balance the composition and create greater depth, as do stones 8 and 9.

▼ **PLAN**

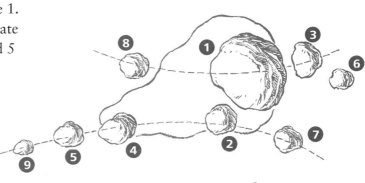

PERSPECTIVE ▼

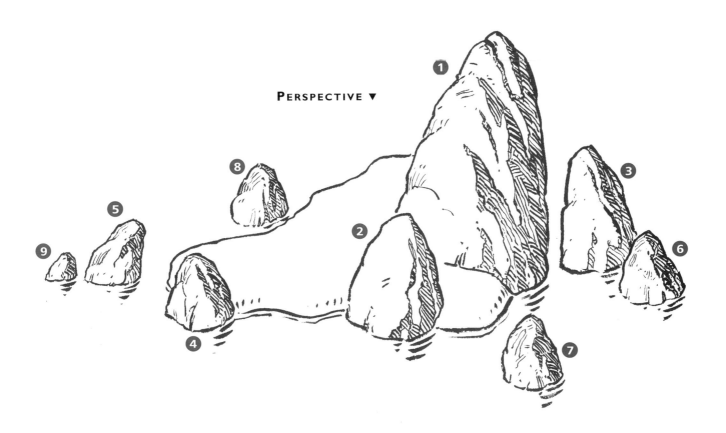

Serpent's Spine

Motivation: The deformation of several mountain peaks that have been exposed to erosional forces, creating plateaus on those peaks.

Application: This type of grouping lends itself well to many locations. It is particularly well suited to sit adjacent to walkways that have traffic flow primarily from one direction.

Description: The lines of force here are horizontal, serpentine, and rising — hence the name Serpent's Spine. Stones 1, 2, and 3 set the tone for the rest of the composition. Stones 4 and 5 cement the relationship. Stones 6 and 7 extend it toward its point of origin. Stones 8 and 9 broaden and deepen the grouping. This arrangement might also be thought of in terms of steppes and steps ascending into the heavens.

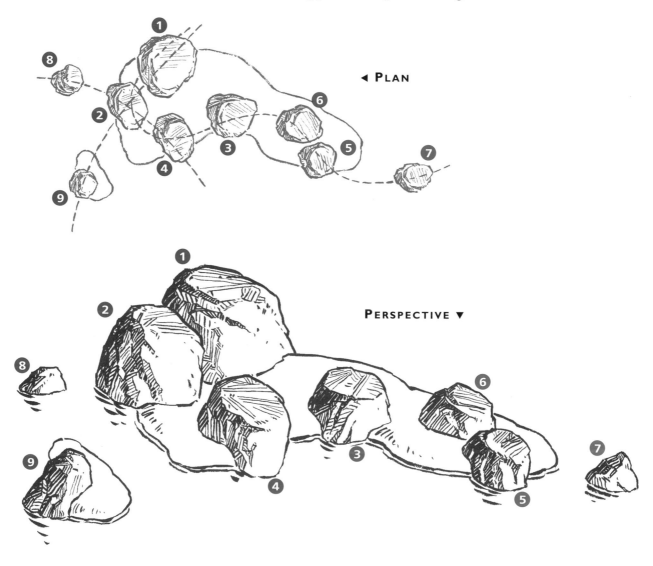

◄ PLAN

PERSPECTIVE ▼

The Tao

Motivation: Limestone monoliths along the Li River in Guilin, China (see page vii).

Application: This composition is well suited to serve as a single focal point or to be seen from a single perspective; it is an admirable meditative device.

Description: The countryside along the Li River is filled with peaks in a variety of heights. It produces an indescribable feeling of tranquillity to be among these towering mountains. The arc formed by the island symbolizes a bend in the river. The first three stones establish the skeleton of the emerging pattern. Stones 4 and 5 consolidate and extend the pattern. Stones 6 and 7 mimic the responsibility of 4 and 5, but in reverse. Stones 8 and 9 take the same approach to consolidation and extension, but do so perpendicularly to the two previous placements. Note that there are essentially three separate groupings created here: 3, 9, and 5; 2, 8, and 7; and 1, 6, and 4.

▼ **PLAN**

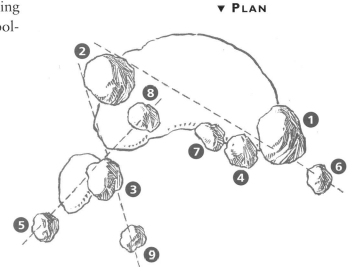

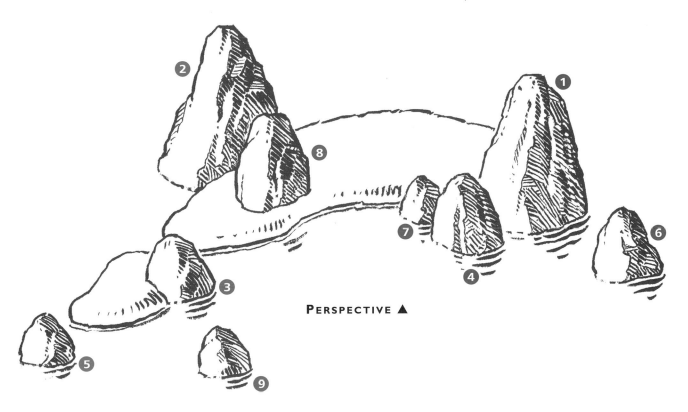

PERSPECTIVE ▲

▶ WORKING WITH A SLOPING PLANE

Troll's Causeway

Motivation: A layer of resistant sedimentary rock exposed on a hillside.

Application: This grouping is best viewed obliquely, so it would work well along a berm adjacent to a walkway. The type of stone will determine the best viewing height, but usually it's best if the group can be seen from below at least stones 1 and 2.

Description: In some landscapes (southern Ohio, for example), you can find great deposits of sandstone that have varying degrees of resistance. As less-resistant areas of surface-level sandstone erode, you are left with horizontal planes jutting into space. The name evokes the mythological troll's propensity for hiding under things; an arrangement like this would serve as a secure highway should a troll pass this way. Stones 1, 2, and 3 basically set the tone, and the subsequent stones serve to reinforce the structure. The external lines of force emanate from within the hill and thrust outward, perpendicular to the vertical.

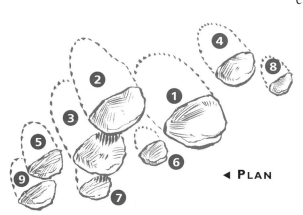

◀ PLAN

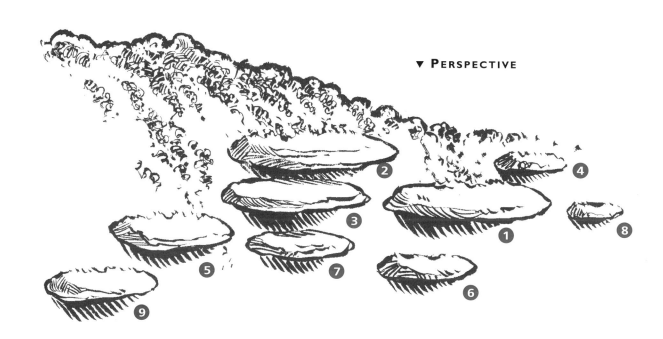

▼ PERSPECTIVE

Petrified Forest

Motivation: As the name implies, a petrified forest. This grouping is also similar to a geological formation found on the edge of the main crater of Mount Haleakala on Maui, Hawaii.

Application: This composition makes a fine intimate, close-up composition; the best height for the tallest stone is 8 to 10 feet (2.4 to 3.1 m) above the ground plane. It's very effective with large plantings and shrub masses mixed with ground covers.

Description: In structure and lines of force, this design is similar to the Pillars of Sumeru (see page 143) but is placed on a sloping plane. Stone 2 should be at 62 percent of the height of stone 1, stone 3 at 62 percent of the height of stone 2, and stone 5 at 31 percent of the height of stone 2. Remember that the ratios of heights need to be based from the same ground plane. The lines of force emanate from points deep in the earth and run parallel to each other. Stones 1, 2, and 3 are, again, seeds to the rest of the formations. Stones 4 and 5 expand it, stones 6 and 7 extend it, and stones 8 and 9 add depth to it.

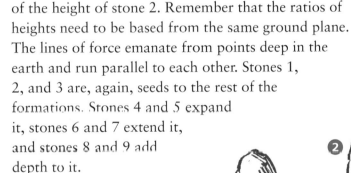

▼ **PLAN**

PERSPECTIVE ▶

Stone Bowl

Motivation: An ancient caldera beginning to emerge from a hillock.

Application: This is an interesting form to use on a hill, because it maintains an interesting form and structure as you circle the hill. When combined with cascading plants, it can be a stabilizing element in the landscape.

Description: This formation is based on an exposed ring of stone near the beginning of the descent into Mount Haleakala. It is similar to Vulcan Necklace (see page 142) but has been covered by earth and is starting to reemerge. Stones 1, 2, and 3 hint at the structure, and the subsequent stones become important in delineating the formation. The internal lines of force emanate from a point below the surface and radiate outward in the form of a bowl — thus the name.

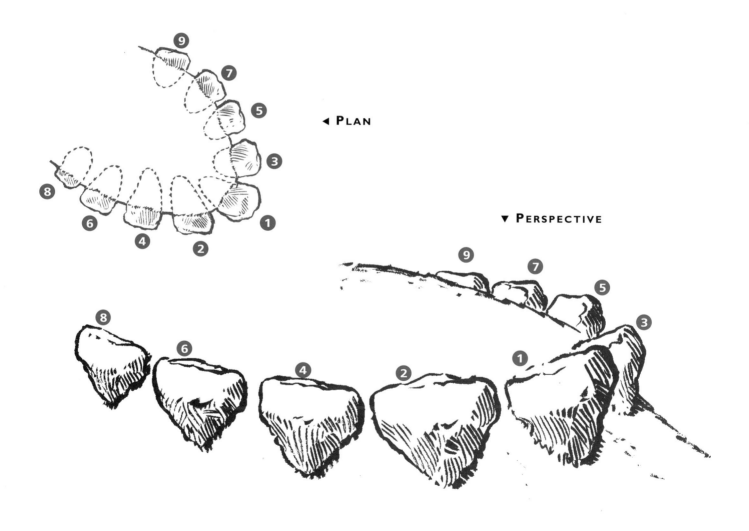

◄ PLAN

▼ PERSPECTIVE

Hag's Reckoning

Motivation: An eroding rock outcropping on the side of a mountain.

Application: This grouping can work from a variety of perspectives, even from above.

Description: This outcropping has the appearance of an old witch's face — a hag's reckoning — when viewed from a certain angle. Stone 1 is the central element, and the others (except for 5) are subordinate to it. Stone 5 serves to reflect and echo the main stone — it should be only about 40 percent of the height of stone 1. The implied planes of all of the other stones should lead directly to the top of stone 1. Stone 2 is placed so that it appears to have been the dominant stone at one time, but has now toppled; it serves to give depth to the composition.

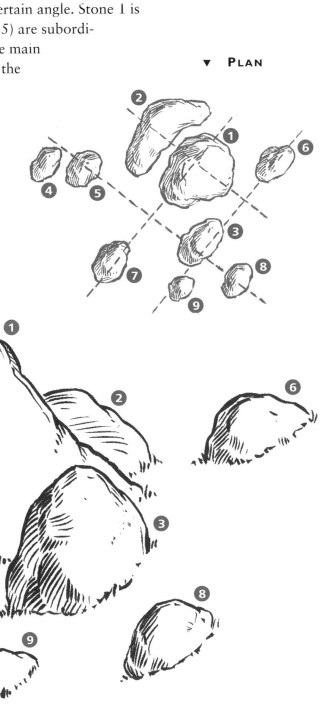

▼ PLAN

PERSPECTIVE ▶

Hedgehog

Motivation: Purely imaginary, although it follows all of the design principles we have derived from nature.

Application: This works from a variety of angles, but it is best used with some kind of connective ground cover. Since it is such a powerful arrangement, it is best to keep its surroundings plain, so that the viewer isn't faced with competing attractions.

Description: Although this grouping isn't based on any form we've ever seen in nature, it works because it *might* exist naturally — because it obeys the principles of nature that we have learned govern natural stone formations. There is a definite unity at play. The base is a ball of hard stone with a superstructure like rays emanating from its core. The less resistant material erodes away, leaving the raylike structure exposed. You can picture these rays coming together at the source of these lines of force. Stones 1, 2, and 3 establish the pattern early on. Stones 4 and 5 add horizontal structure to the group. Stones 6 and 7 add depth, and stones 8 and 9 reinforce depth for the entire group.

▼ **PLAN**

PERSPECTIVE ▶

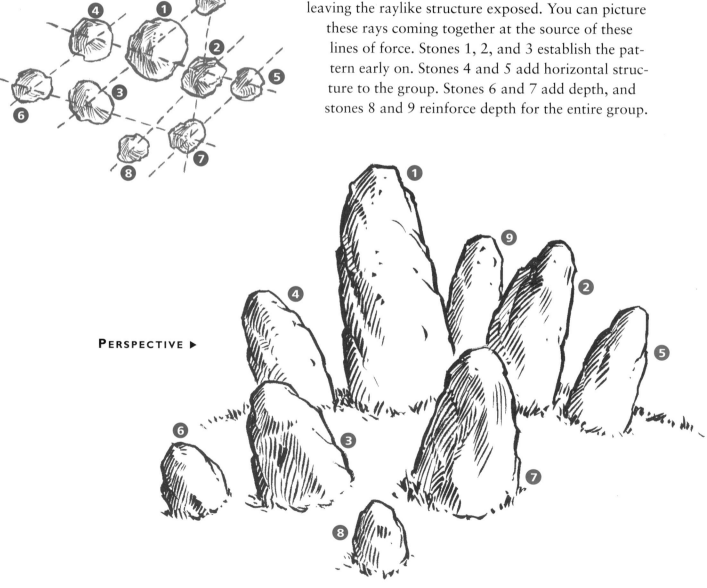

▶ WORKING WITH A TRANSITION ZONE

The Lighthouse

Motivation: The guardianship of lighthouses — not a motivation of nature, certainly, but an attempt by humankind to dominate our relationship with nature.

Application: This arrangement works from many directions. It could be used in any environment in which a sloping plane joins a flat one (such as a shrub bed joining a ground cover).

Description: In nature, it is highly unusual to find this type of pinnacle on the shore of a body of water. The closest to it may be the Rock of Gibraltar. The line of force is singular and upright, pulling the implied planes of all of the subordinate stones upward like so many strings on a maypole. Stones 1, 2, and 3 make the clear connection between the sloping shore and the flat plane of water, ground, or planting bed. Stones 4 and 5 reinforce that connection. Stone 6 stabilizes the arrangement by anchoring it to the shore, and stone 7 continues the transition into the water. Stones 8 and 9 bring the whole composition forward and give it greater depth.

◀ **PLAN**

PERSPECTIVE ▶

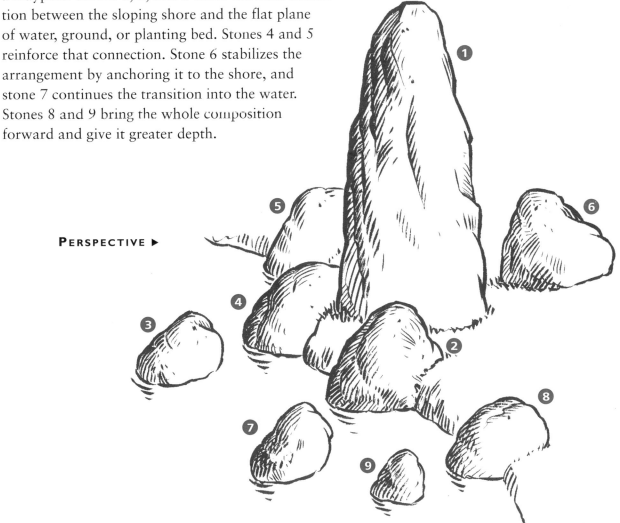

Our designs for transition zones are all featured at water's edge, the transition zone between shore and water. Truth be told, stonescapes are exceptionally well-suited for landscapes with ponds or small streams — the mixture of land, water, and stone casts a familiar picture of the stone formations we frequently see in the wilds. However, you can mimic the water's-edge transition zone with a stone grouping leading from a raised garden bed to the level yard. You can even set two or three of the larger stones of a grouping within the boundaries of a deck, cut holes in the planking for the stones to poke through, and lead the rest of the stones down into the yard for the same effect.

Reclining Dragon

Motivation: The rocky shore of a lake.

Application: This, like Sinking Mountains (page 157), is best viewed from the perspective of the flat plane, although an oblique perspective can work as well.

Description: When people use stone to represent the shore of a body of water, they usually make the mistake of using rocks of the same sizes and dimensions and placing them all on the edge of that "shore." The metaphor of a reclining dragon intimates the range of sizes and relative locations of stones that actually occur on a typical shore. Stone 1 is the dragon's pelvis. Stone 2 is its right rear leg, extending into the water. Stone 3 is the dragon's head, and stone 4 is the butt of the dragon's tail, which lies deep in the water. Stone 5 is its right front leg and stones 6 and 8 are its long neck. Stone 7 is part of its left rear leg, holding it to the shore, while stone 9 is part of its right rear leg, extending into the water.

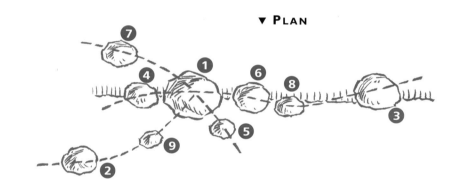

▼ **PLAN**

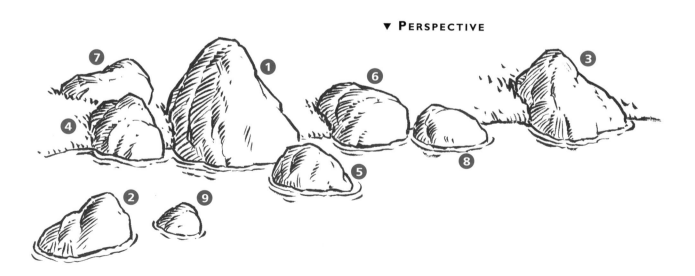

▼ **PERSPECTIVE**

Sinking Mountains

Motivation: An eroding mountain range starting to sink into the ocean.

Application: This grouping works best viewed from somewhere out in the flat plane.

Description: This grouping is similar to Crying Mountain (page 141) and Swimming Dragon (at left) but is anchored on a shore. The internal lines of force descend into the water (flat plane). Stones 1, 2, and 3 establish the design. Stones 4 and 5 reinforce the connection with the flat plane. Stone 6 anchors the composition on the sloping plane, while stone 7 extends the reach of the group. Stones 8 and 9 create foreground interest.

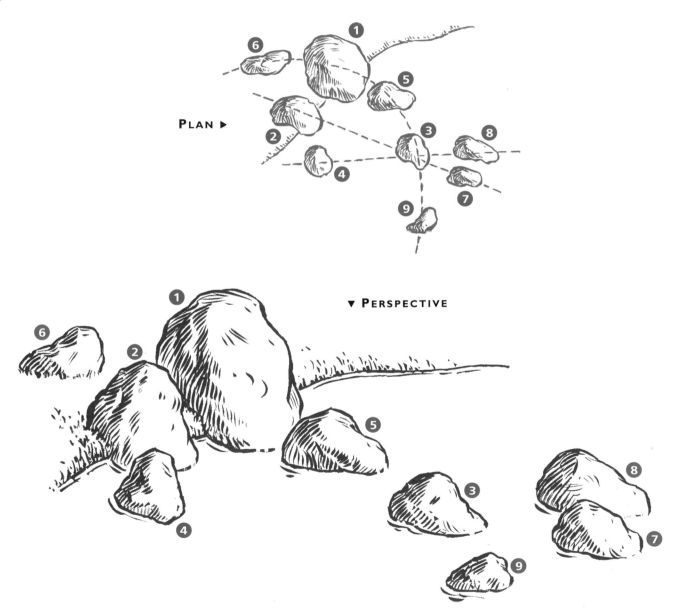

PLAN ▶

▼ PERSPECTIVE

Rabbit's Rump

Motivation: A typical peninsula extending into a body of water.

Application: This grouping works from a variety of perspectives; the only bad one is looking down toward the flat plane, which can be blocked by stone {00}.

Description: This grouping's descending hump, along with the breaking-up action of the stone below, is what happens to a peninsula as it is subjected over time to the heavy erosion caused by crashing waves. The internal line of force here is directed upward toward the rabbit's rump, following the energy of the waves. Stones 1, 2, and 3 set the stage. Stones 4 and 5 expand the grouping in width. Stones 6 and 7 extend the group outward along the lines of force. Stones 8 and 9 reinforce the dynamics of the grouping.

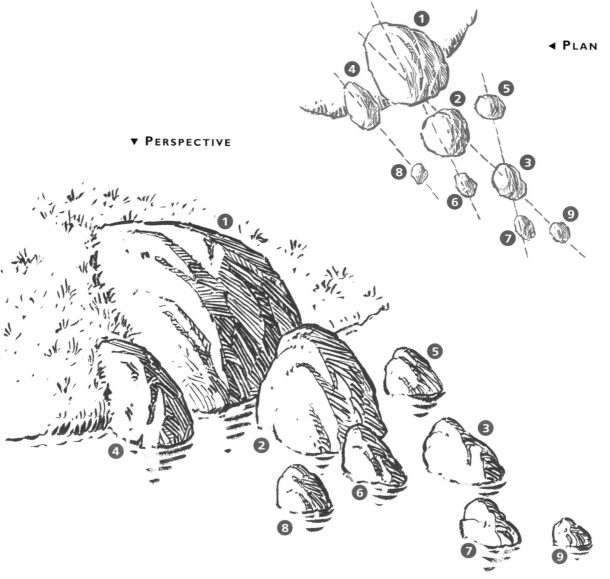

◄ **PLAN**

▼ **PERSPECTIVE**

Dragon's Tail

Motivation: Like the Hedgehog (page 154), this design finds its roots in the imagination but is based upon the principles of natural formations.

Application: This dynamic grouping works well from nearly all perspectives, regardless of the number of stones used.

Description: Here we've attempted to represent a dinosaur with spikes on its tail that died eons ago and was buried by the ages; its fossil tail is now starting to be exposed. This arrangement is particularly interesting because the form looks quite different at each step of its evolution. Stones 1, 2, and 3 don't even hint at what is to come. Stones 4 and 5 add some dimension but still don't give away the surprise. Stones 6 and 7 serve simply to extend and anchor the composition, while stones 8 and 9 become the missing links.

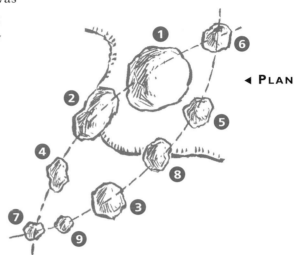

◄ **PLAN**

PERSPECTIVE ►

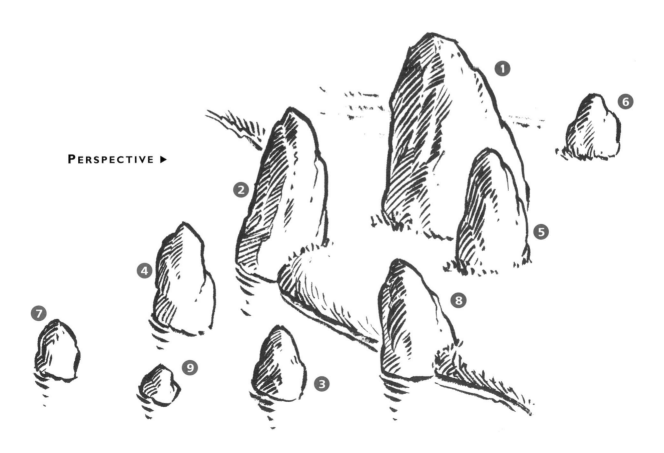

Appendix

RESOURCES

Stonescape Design Services

Thea authors are available for collaboration on design, supply, and/or installtion of stonescapes. For information, contact Richard L. Dubé at Environmental Information & Design, Inc., or Frederick C. Campbell at Gnome Landscapes, Design & Masonry.

Environmental Information & Design, Inc.
Richard L. Dubé, APLD
1651 Caulks Ferry Road
Lexington, SC 29072
(803) 356-3672
E-mail: naturedan@aol.com
Offers service internationally. Also available for workshops and lectures.

Gnome Landscapes, Design & Masonry
Rick Campbell
P.O. Box 66803
Falmouth, ME 04105
(207) 781-2955
E-mail: GnomeLDM@aol.com
Offers service in the northeastern United States.

Masahiko Seko
RR #3, Box 530
Gorham, ME 04038
(207) 929-5924
Offers service throughout the United States.

Stōn Wûrks
Rick Anderson
4464 Devine Street, Suite I-10
Columbia, SC 29205
(803) 513-3958
Stone artist and stone broker. Offers service throughout the United States.

Stone Suppliers

Nature's Way Nursery
1451 Pleasant Hill Road
Harrisburg, PA 17112
(717) 545-4555
Landscape stone and viewing (suiseki) *stone. Will ship within United States and Canada.*

Mountain West — Colorado Aggregate
4212 South Highway 191
Rexburg, ID 83440
(800) 727-9959
Fax: (800) 254-8886
Decorative pebbles, lava rocks, and boulders as well as various landscaping materials. Offers service internationally.

Price's Block & Brick
Randy Price
358 Cactus Road
Gilbert, SC 29054
Stone supplier for South Carolina only.

Southwest Stone, Inc.
11351 East 36th Street North
Tulsa, OK 74116
(918) 438-3777
Offers service throughout the United States.

Winters' Stone Sales
1562 Old Leicester Highway
Asheville, NC 28806
(704) 252-4718
Landscape boulders and decorative stone. Will ship only within the continental United States.

ORGANIZATIONS

The North American Viewing Stone Society
P.O. Box 27
Broomall, PA 19008-0027
Promotes suiseki *and education in the finer aspects of the art form of viewing stones.*

Index

Page references in *italicized* text indicate illustrations or photographs.

PHOTOGRAPHY CREDITS

Other Storey Titles You Will Enjoy

Landscaping Makes Cents: A Homeowner's Guide to Adding Value and Beauty to Your Propery, by Frederick C. Campbell and Richard L. Dubé. Add substantial investment value and beauty to a home with this guide to landscape design. Explains how to create a landscape plan, determine a budget, choose a contractor, and achieve substantial financial return on a limited budget. Includes tips for the beginning landscaper and handy checklists and charts to ensure the successful completion of any project. 176 pages. Paperback. ISBN 0-88266-948-6.

Step-by-Step Outdoor Stonework, edited by Mike Lawrence. Over twenty easy-to-build projects for your patio and garden, including walls, arches, bird baths, sun dials, and fountains. Includes information on estimating costs, selecting tools and materials, and preparing the site. 96 pages. Paperback. ISBN 0-88266-891-9.

Stonescaping: A Guide to Using Stone in Your Garden, by Jan Whitner. A thorough guide to incorporating stone into many garden features, including paths, steps, walls, ponds, and rock gardens. More than 20 designs are included. 176 pages. Paperback. ISBN 0-88266-755-6.

The Feng Shui Garden: Design Your Garden for Health, Wealth, and Happiness, by Gill Hale. A fascinating exploration of gardening in accordance with Feng Shui principles. Readers will learn how to create balanced outdoor spaces that positively influence health, relationships, and happiness. Four-color photography and illustrated garden plans of balanced window boxes, roof gardens and terraces; garden paths, statuary, and outbuildings are also included. 128 pages. Paperback. ISBN 1-58017-022-6.

Stonework: Techniques and Projects, by Charles McRaven. This complete guide includes fully illustrated, step-by-step instructions for 22 projects, including walls, porches, pools, seats, waterfalls, and even a bridge. Advice on gathering and handling stone and hiring stonemasons is also included. 192 pages. Paperback. ISBN 0-88266-976-1.

Building with Stone, by Charles McRaven. An introduction to the art and craft of creating stone structures, including finding stone, tools to use, and step-by-step instructions for projects such as walls, buttresses, fireplaces, a barbecue pit, a stone dam, and even a home or barn. Also includes instruction on proper restoration techniques for stone structures. 192 pages. Paperback. ISBN 0-88266-550-2.

Building Stone Walls, by John Vivian. A step-by-step guide to building both freestanding and retaining walls. Includes equipment requirements, instructions for creating wall foundations, ways to cope with drainage problems, and hints for incorporating gates, fences, and stiles. 112 pages. Paperback. ISBN 0-88266-074-8.

Waterscaping: Plants and Ideas for Natural and Created Water Gardens, by Judy Glattstein. Packed with information on moist and wet spot gardening, pool installation, container water gardens, and border treatments. 192 pages. Paperback. ISBN 0-88266-606-1.

These and other Storey books are available at your bookstore, farm store, garden center, or directly from Storey Books, Schoolhouse Road, Pownal, Vermont 05261, or by calling 1-800-441-5700. Or visit our Web site at www.storey.com.